STEPHEN POWELL is a journal  twenty-seven years. He has lived except Antarctica and brings to hi perspective. His reporting has inc and Brazil's transition from milita ᴗᵣᵤᵤᵧ. ᴵᴵᵉ ᴵᴵᵛᵉˢ in Portugal.

WALKING
EUROPE'S
REFLECTIONS
ON PORTUGAL EDGE

STEPHEN POWELL

SilverWood

Published in 2021 by SilverWood Books

SilverWood Books Ltd
14 Small Street, Bristol, BS1 1DE, United Kingdom
www.silverwoodbooks.co.uk

ISBN 978-1-80042-060-1 (paperback)
ISBN 978-1-80042-061-8 (ebook)

British Library Cataloguing in Publication Data
A CIP catalogue record for this book is
available from the British Library

Page design and typesetting by SilverWood Books

To the warm-hearted people of Portugal who made me fall in love with the country

Contents

ATLANTIC
OCEAN

Santiago de
Compostela

S P A I N

Puebla de
Sanabria

Rio de
Onor

Bragança

Chaves

BRAGA

Guimarães Fafe

Peso da
Régua Pocinho

PORTO Pinhão

Viseu

Guarda

Coimbra

Figueira
da Foz

P
O
R
T
U
G
A
L

Fátima
Tomar

Santarém

Águas de
Moura Évora

LISBON

Setúbal

Caba
Beja

Mértola

Alcoutim

Aljezur Barranco-
de-Velho

Vila do Silves
Bispo

Faro

Cape St Sagres
Vincent

100 km

Introduction

Three decades ago now, I received an invitation to work in Portugal as a foreign correspondent. I turned the opportunity down because it cut against the grain of what I wanted to do with my life at that point. When the chance arose, I had been reporting from Brazil for nearly five years and I was homesick for my native land, Britain.

If I'm honest, there was another reason. I couldn't shake off the feeling that I might find Portugal dull after the buzz of Brazil, with its distinctive brand of colour, chaos and raw energy. The commercial dynamism of São Paulo, the burning of the Amazon rainforests, the samba parades of Rio de Janeiro – the news file out of Brazil was varied and vibrant. What would I write about from Portugal? So I said "no" to a Lisbon posting.

In 2018 I felt in a quite different frame of mind. I finally said "yes" to Portugal and went under my own steam to discover the country. There is often, I believe, a residual element of mystery about why we get called to a certain place at a certain time. I can't fully explain the pull to Portugal. But I know that after the dreadful business of Britain voting to leave the European Union, I felt a restlessness in my soul. I wanted to see how another West European country that had lost an empire was faring in the 21st century. How did the Portuguese feel about themselves and their diminished role in the world? Just what were the big themes in Portugal's past and present?

As I prepared for my journey, I had conversations with people who had returned from Portugal or were planning to go there. It seemed as if the world and his wife were beating a path to Portugal. Still, looking at the map, I decided it would be easy to steer clear of crowded beaches and explore the backcountry in autumn and winter, to avoid the summer heat.

I had a plan – to walk the length of Portugal, from top right to bottom left. There was something about the size of the country that appealed to the walker in me. It looked doable, a challenge but not an absurd one that could be tackled in easy stages. This would be the longest walk I'd ever attempted, but the idea lodged in my head as one clearly defined package and it never occurred to me to travel in any other way. I more or less made up the route as I went along, though there were a number of places that I knew I had to see.

The overarching framework, then, was one long walk and the primary aim was to learn about Portugal. Sometimes in this book, in the interest of deeper understanding, I have focused on a subject and temporarily set aside the travelogue. On three occasions, I have devoted chapters to big topics – the Portuguese Empire, the historic relationship between Portugal and England, and the country's leading modern poet. The sub-title of this book is "Reflections on Portugal" and the digressions explore themes not easily contained within the narrative of my zigzag path.

I love Europe and am both fascinated by its past and intrigued about its future. My hope is that readers will learn something about one small European country that, although much visited, is perhaps not deeply understood. Portugal's distinctiveness is hard to capture in just a few words – hence the book.

On my walk, I met kindness at every turn. You will discover, if you stick with me, that my journey through Portugal was for me a life-changing passage.

CHAPTER 1

To Portugal, via Bordeaux and Bilbao

All journeys have to start somewhere, and I decided to begin this account in Bordeaux, France. As a kind of meditation before the walk began, I resolved to pay my respects to one of Portugal's Second World War heroes, Aristides de Sousa Mendes. This Portuguese diplomat defied the orders of his government in Lisbon. In 1940, when he was consul in Bordeaux, he issued visas to thousands of people, many of them Jews, wishing to flee the advancing armies of Nazi Germany. Holocaust historian Yehuda Bauer has called his feat "perhaps the largest rescue operation by a single individual during the Holocaust".

Sousa Mendes acted in defiance of an order called Circular 14, a directive to diplomats issued by the Portuguese dictatorship of António Salazar. This instructed diplomats to deny safe haven to refugees, including Jews and Russians. By granting the visas Sousa Mendes enabled thousands to flee first to Spain and then into officially neutral Portugal. From there they were free to make onward journeys to other parts of the world. Those who managed to escape from occupied France with his visas included the surrealist painter Salvador Dali and his wife, and some members of the Rothschild banking family.

Defending his actions, Sousa Mendes told his government he was "obeying the dictates of humanity that distinguish between neither race nor nationality". Sousa Mendes was a Portuguese aristocrat – his twin brother César had briefly been foreign minister – but his defiance of Salazar cost him dear. The dictator ended his diplomatic career and cut his pay. For a while he and his family ate at a soup kitchen set up by Lisbon's Jewish community.

Today Sousa Mendes is widely honoured as a hero. In Bordeaux, a statue of him graces a park, the Esplanade Charles de Gaulle, where Bordelais picnic on the grass or sit by the edge of a pool while a jet fountain spurts high in the air. The statue is a bronze bust of the diplomat in jacket and tie. The inscription reads: "Aristides de Sousa Mendes, 1885 – 1954, Consul du Portugal à Bordeaux, En juin 1940 sa signature a sauvé 30,000 réfugiés."

What began in my head as a tribute to a Portuguese hero turned into an exercise in taking the pulse of two cities on the Atlantic shore, Bordeaux and Bilbao. This made sense to me, rather than going straight to Portugal with no idea of the vibe further along the Atlantic coast.

It was my first visit to Bordeaux and its beauty and vibrancy made a strong impression. The waterfront along the Garonne River is surely one of the great urban sights of Western Europe. Photos I have seen don't really do it justice. The combination of the river and that long frontage of elegant 18th century buildings stir the soul.

Bordeaux is listed as a World Heritage Site by UNESCO which praises the city's "exceptional urban and architectural unity and coherence". It has more protected buildings than anywhere in France except for Paris. The city's wealth grew out of the wine business and out of Atlantic trade in general. On the eve of the French Revolution in 1789, Bordeaux was France's most important colonial port. It controlled nearly half of the country's trade and sent twice as many ships to the West Indies as rivals Nantes or Marseille.

Looking at a map of the city's public transport system, I was struck by the names of tram stations. In their quest for names, the planners have rounded up the usual French suspects like Jean Jaurès and Alfred de Vigny. But they have also brought a broad geographical awareness to the task and looked east and west for inspiration. Tram line A features Stalingrad, line B Brandenburg and New York, and line C Cracovie and Lycée Václav Havel. This cosmopolitan naming helps to give Bordeaux a feel of openness to the world. In a Europe more politically evolved than it is today, Bordeaux would make a fine European Union capital.

I liked the honesty on display in the city's Musée d'Aquitaine, which aims to relate the story of Bordeaux and Aquitaine. With its model wooden ships and soundtracks of the sea, the museum strongly evokes the city's maritime heritage. What struck me most was that it had a big section on the history of slavery, which gives an overview of the Atlantic trade and explains its relevance to Bordeaux. It says that between the 15th and 19th centuries between 11 and 13 million human beings left African shores as slaves. An estimated 1.7 million Africans did not survive the appalling conditions of the Middle Passage.

The museum quotes British historian Hugh Thomas on the price of a slave in the West African port of Ouidah in 1767: 600 litres of brandy or 25 guns or 40 iron bars or 10 lengths of Indian cotton cloth or 100,000 cowry shells.

Although Bordeaux dealers did buy some slaves, the museum says that generally the city benefitted indirectly from slavery. "Bordeaux's wealth came from the trade in goods produced by slave labour, rather than from the slave trade itself." The city could have opted to stay silent on this delicate theme and concentrate on more glorious subjects. But it chose to address slavery squarely. Portugal played an important role in the Atlantic slave trade and I wondered how their museums treated this subject.

From Bordeaux I took a coach to Bilbao, in the lush green Basque Country of northern Spain, and once again I was forcefully struck by the sheer energy of the city. It seemed somehow both vigorous and relaxed.

I went into a bar in the old part of town that sold *pintxos* or small snacks. A couple came in with their daughter, who was probably about two years old. They plonked her on the bar counter and Mum enjoyed a beer. A middle-aged barmaid blew kisses at the young girl and generally made a fuss of her. Surveying the scene, I knew beyond any doubt that I was no longer in my home country.

The very name Bilbao for me has a grittiness about it and historically there has been a very gritty side to the city. Its population grew rapidly in the 19th and early 20th centuries with a port focused on exporting iron. Bilbao reinvented itself with a most imaginative vision of urban renewal. At the heart of this renewal is the Guggenheim Museum which celebrated its 21st birthday in October 2018, the month after my visit. But really it came of age some time ago, symbolising great architecture and a regenerated Bilbao around the world.

The Guggenheim Bilbao immediately became my favourite modern building. The museum has an expansive, confident, welcoming feel that can only be experienced by going to see it. The building, on the banks of the River Nervión, is a wondrous sculpture of titanium, glass and stone. Frank Gehry, the Canadian-American architect, says that in his design he was inspired partly by ships' sails and by the city's maritime tradition.

He explains on the museum's audio guide: "I was just trying to get a sense of movement in my building, a subtle kind of energy. And making a building that has a sense of movement appeals to me because it knits into the larger fabric of the movement of the city."

On the approach to the Guggenheim is artist Jeff Koons' playful *Puppy*, a 13-metre high topiary sculpture of a West Highland terrier carpeted in flowers. I warmed to Bilbao.

So, wending my way to Portugal overland I encountered two cities on the Atlantic shore that seemed in very good heart. From Bilbao I took a night bus to Puebla de Sanabria, a Spanish town in the region of Castile and León that I had earmarked as the start of my walk. It was 15 kilometres from the Portuguese border. I had done no research beyond booking a room, but Puebla de Sanabria turned out to be a most engaging place, a delightful medieval hill town with narrow cobbled streets. Cascades of flowers on the front of some dwellings softened the austerity of the stone. In one street I stumbled across a Michelin-listed mycological restaurant and treated myself to veal tail with ceps followed by one of the best desserts ever, a lemon cream with extraordinary depth of flavour.

I was well set up to walk to Portugal the next day.

CHAPTER 2

First Steps on the Road to Sagres

I left the Spanish town of Puebla de Sanabria in late September under a cloudless sky, walking through hill country on a minor road with barely any traffic. I carried a rucksack, containing a Big Agnes one-man tent, a sleeping bag, waterproofs, a Michelin map of north Portugal, a few books, some socks, spare shirt, underwear and not much else. When I stopped by a fountain for a mid-morning snack, the sound of a woodpecker at work echoed through the trees – it was a gentle, bucolic start to my Iberian walk.

South of the hamlet of Ungilde the road entered a conifer plantation and I chafed at being enclosed in this monotonous world. When a car appeared in the midst of this soulless landscape and the driver offered me a lift, I recognised this at once as Temptation playing a very old game. I graciously declined.

Sometime in the mid-afternoon I entered a Spanish village that seemed dead as a doornail. Without any announcement at all, beyond some bunting strung above the road, this sleepy settlement turned into a Portuguese village. On the Portuguese side of the border there were some signs of life – a café with tables and chairs outside offered the chance of a beer and conversation with the locals. This is an unusual village. Astride an international border, it has to cope with two time zones. When I arrived in September it was GMT +2 on the Spanish side, Rihonor de Castilla, and GMT +1 on the Portuguese side, Rio de Onor.

I wanted to ease myself slowly into Portugal so I checked into the local campsite for two nights. I found a novel use for a can of fish, wielding it as a hammer to bang tent pegs into the hard Portuguese earth. In the campsite's reception area I saw on display black-and-white photos of villagers. They were all, without exception, wrinkled elders with faces full of character. By entering the northeast corner of Portugal I had effectively come into an extended old people's home, with no one under retirement age in sight.

In this border village I could pick up immediately the vibe of interactions between the Spanish and Portuguese. I sat in a little restaurant one day in Rio de Onor and listened to an exchange that conveyed the flavour of the relationship between the two Iberian nations in just eight words.

Male Spanish customer to Portuguese waitress: "La cuenta, por favor."

The waitress, replying to this request for the bill: "Sim Senhor, a conta."

The refusal of both parties in this conversation to use the language of the other has parallels, I am sure, in other parts of the world, but it is central to the Spain/Portugal dynamic that the Spanish do not generally trouble to learn the testing language of their neighbour. The Portuguese, on the other hand, have no difficulty understanding Spanish. We all know that people appreciate it when visiting foreigners make an attempt to speak their language. The Portuguese, I was to discover, are pleased as punch when a foreigner speaks their tongue. Warm compliments come at once and that is part of the country's charm.

During my stay in Rio de Onor I gravitated mainly towards the café at the centre of the village, ordered some beers at one euro a bottle and just let the mood of the place wash over me. The locals were ever so friendly and conversation flowed. It is a community-run café, in what used to be a customs officer's house, and people take turns to work there. On one occasion a man who had spent time in the Portuguese army served me. He had been in the former Atlantic colony of Cape Verde, a group of nine inhabited islands, helping to guard an air base.

"I can still remember the names of all the islands," he said and proceeded to reel them off with no hesitation. When you cross an international border in Europe it isn't only the language that changes, the local sense of world geography shifts too.

As I sat drinking the place in, I was able to do people-watching of an unusual kind. The café is right next to vegetable plots dotted with scarecrows. Wheelbarrows trundled past me pushed by ageing villagers. An old woman with a limp hobbled past at one point, gamely pushing a barrow. There were moments when I almost felt I was intruding on private grief, watching the death throes of an entire village.

In the literature on Portugal are accounts of Rio de Onor's community-focused way of life, but I quickly discovered that this is passing into history since all the young have fled in search of jobs and only the old are left. In the village population of about 70 people I don't think there is anyone under 60. Travellers say it is the same story right across the northeastern corner of Portugal, in the Montesinho Natural Park and beyond.

Someone might set up an eco-tourism venture here or buy a particularly charming stone house there, but without jobs or any young blood it is hard to see a future for these villages. I found myself pondering that one important skill set in these parts was perhaps similar to that of the hospice worker, the facilitator of serene and dignified death.

Straying from my usual perch in the café, I spent a little time sitting by myself and reading. An old man walking slowly with a stick from the direction of Spain came and sat beside me. He introduced himself as Francisco Augusto Preto. At the age of 93, he said, he was the oldest man in the village. He lived with his 88-year-old wife. They had two daughters and six grandchildren who had settled elsewhere in Portugal. He had always lived in Rio de Onor, working as a farmer, and he reminisced about his earlier days when he helped to drive livestock, sometimes three times a month, to the town of Braganza. This entailed a 3 a.m. start, to do the 50-kilometre round trip in a day.

The man from the café who had been a soldier also told me about working as a drover on the road to Braganza. I picked up from both of them a vivid sense of the crushing tedium of the job. At the same time, I thought, they communicated a sense of loss. Rio de Onor no longer had any livestock and it negotiated its place in the broader scheme of things from a position of reduced status.

Both men also spoke at length on what seemed to be the burning topic in Rio de Onor – the depredations of wild deer in the village vegetable plots. "They particularly like the sweetcorn," said my 93-year-old friend sadly. The man from the café told me to listen out at night for the sound of rutting stags because it was now the mating season.

I had never heard rutting stags before and lying in my tent trying to sleep I found the noise quite remarkable. It is a deep primeval bellow that seems to come from the bowels of the earth. When I walked out of Rio de Onor at sunrise after two nights in the village the rutting stags were still bellowing. At intervals, six shots rang out through the morning air. Villagers had told me that there was some illicit culling of these protected animals. Was this a deer hunter?

Once again, after a few kilometres, the little road entered a conifer forest. Once again, a driver stopped and offered me a ride. I searched for a phrase to explain succinctly why I didn't need a lift and out of my head popped "I am walking to Sagres."

"To Sagres?" exclaimed the driver, clapping his hands once to savour this absurd notion. He put his foot down and I was alone again in the desolation of conifers. (I put this forward as the right collective noun. If the English language can accommodate an "unkindness of ravens" there must surely be space for a "desolation of conifers".)

Sagres, I should explain, is a household word in Portugal. It is a parish at the southwestern end of Portugal and continental Europe and it has given its name to a ubiquitous Portuguese beer. For centuries Sagres was an important destination for European pilgrims because the headland was associated with St Vincent. These days Sagres attracts surfers, walkers and bird-watchers who go to ride the waves or to see the high cliffs and the eagles, storks, falcons and vultures. I hadn't worked out how many kilometres I expected to cover before reaching Sagres. Sometimes it's better not to know.

Swapping a settled existence at home for a long walk through a foreign land is a profound change of rhythm. In this first stage of my journey I had a distinct sense of fiddling with the cultural dials to get onto the local wavelength better. I have a good command of Brazilian Portuguese but I struggled at times with Portugal's variety of the language.

I hiked the first Portuguese section, the 25 kilometres from Rio de Onor to Braganza, in a happy, carefree spirit. I was unencumbered by livestock, of course. Cafés, and there are many in Portugal, are an obvious way of punctuating a walk. I discovered that some Portuguese cafés, at least in the rural areas, have rhythms rather different from British pubs. I stopped for a drink in the village of Varge at the end of the morning. Shortly after midday the café owner ushered me out. He was closing, he said, so that he could get some lunch. His sense of priorities put a smile on my face.

In Braganza I checked into a hostel where a young woman from Armenia greeted me at reception. She seemed generally happy with her lot in Portugal, but she commented ruefully that whereas in Armenia you could find some store somewhere open at the dead of night, this was not the case among the Portuguese.

Braganza is largely modern but the old part, clustered around the castle, has charm. People still live in the narrow streets within the walls of the surrounding citadel, built by Portugal's first king, Afonso Henriques, in 1130. His son Sancho built the castle itself a little later, so the place has pedigree.

What struck me was how this medieval castle gave a sense of the strong historical bonds that developed between Portugal and Africa. Alongside the usual swords and suits of armour, its military museum displayed wooden statuettes from Angola. A war memorial outside on one side of the castle records the names of more than 200 local men killed in Portugal's African colonial wars between 1961 and 1974. It was a stark reminder of the blood and treasure that Portugal invested in a now vanished empire. In all, about 9,000 Portuguese died in those wars which at their peak cost the country about 40 percent of its GDP.

I took in Braganza's Graça Morais Contemporary Art Centre, named for a local painter. Much of the centre focused on her art, but I was drawn to an exhibition on the work of Brazil's Sebastião Salgado, one of the great photographers of our time. Salgado came to my attention when I worked in Brazil in the 1980s with his extraordinary images of anthills of gold prospectors at Serra Pelada in the Amazon. There was one searing image from Serra Pelada in the exhibition, showing a muscular shirtless man grasping the barrel of a gun held by a soldier. The confrontation neatly mirrored tensions created by military rule in Brazil from the 1960s to 1980s.

As a correspondent who has worked in both Brazil and Africa I found it easy to relate to Portugal's sense of connection to the wider world. In this way I was feeling very much at home.

From Braganza, my plan was to head towards the Atlantic shore, moving from east to west through the northernmost regions of Portugal. Michelin maps show green lines following roads deemed to be picturesque. So far I had not been on any such road (too many conifers?), but now nearly all the route of about 100 kilometres between Braganza and Braga in northwest Portugal was adorned with green.

I set out from Braganza under clear skies and walked through a landscape of rolling wooded hills given character by stately chestnut trees. I passed occasional plantings of young trees and there was no doubting the role of chestnuts in the local economy.

I walked until it felt time to stop. A village called Vila Verde came into view and from afar I could hear music echoing through the countryside. I followed the sound to its source in the centre of the village and discovered a lively outdoor party. If I had been more attuned to Portugal and the Christian calendar I would have guessed the reason for the festivities. A Portuguese reveller had to explain. The date was September 29 and this was a party for Archangel Michael. A band played on an outdoor stage and some villagers danced while others looked on or drank.

The partygoer, a friendly middle-aged Portuguese man who spoke to me in French, offered me space on his lawn to put up my tent. José was his name. I retired early but my tent was right next door to the party. A great rhythmic thumping continued until three o'clock in the morning when someone decided that Archangel Michael had been sufficiently honoured for one year and the music stopped.

Over breakfast I chatted to José and his French wife Catherine. We talked in French and a classic tale of Portugal's rural north unfolded. José spent his early years in Vila Verde, but then his family left Portugal in 1969.

"We left clandestinely, through the mountains, a family of 10 of us on foot," said José. The family group included a one-year-old baby. After reaching Spain they travelled by train on to France, part of a great exodus of Portuguese people during the stifling rule of Salazar.

Catherine emphasised the scale of the emigration over the years. "All of these houses you see in the village, 80 percent of the owners live in France or Spain or Switzerland and they come here only for the holidays," she said. Certainly Portuguese villages in the north can feel drained of life and residents lament the absence of the young.

For the next three days I walked westwards, towards the city of Chaves, and kept meeting friendship and hospitality. Little gestures can mean a lot. Once a young man stopped his car, gave me some grapes and offered the advice that a rest area for drivers a few kilometres ahead would make a good place to camp. His gift reminded me of Nagorno-Karabakh in the Caucasus where three years earlier, at the same time of year, village women had given me bunches of grapes. I enjoy walking through wine country at harvest time.

In Chaves I paid for a bed and savoured this engaging city. Chaves has one great gift from history, a 16-arched Roman bridge built in AD 104 in the reign of the Emperor Trajan. There is no great fanfare about this structure, certainly no tourist tat, just a fine 140m bridge doing its thing as it has done for nearly two millennia. The bridge is closed to motorised traffic but integrated into the town plan and you can stroll across at your leisure.

From Chaves my route turned south. On the morning of October 5 I reached the town of Vila Pouca de Aguiar and went into a general store to buy bread rolls. The woman in the shop said she had no bread and added the word *friado*. That stumped me and then I realised that she had swallowed a syllable, as the Portuguese so often do. She was telling me that it was a *feriado*, a holiday, hence the absence of bread.

So what was the holiday for? The question visibly rattled her; she clearly had no idea. Later, out in the town, a brisk young man on a bicycle dressed in all the modern kit explained that Portugal was celebrating the end of the monarchy in 1910. So, if you are ever in Portugal on October 5 and cannot find bread, do not fret. The country is not falling apart, just commemorating the birth of the Republic.

My exchange with the woman in the shop reminded me that I still had language work to do. I started learning Portuguese in 1986 when Reuters sent me as a correspondent to São Paulo, Brazil's economic capital. Luckily I had been studying Spanish in London and that helped. I asked the company for a week off to study Portuguese ahead of my posting. I seem to remember they gave me two days off and when I arrived in Brazil I needed some tutoring, to dip my toe into commodity reporting. A rather formal woman gave me lessons and I remember asking her "How do you say in Portuguese 'What is your estimate of the soybean crop?'"

"Qual é sua estimativa da colheita de soja?" was her answer. The phrase is engraved in my memory, though since leaving Brazil I haven't found much use for it. I spoke Portuguese every day in my work for nearly five years and became reasonably proficient. Marriage to a Brazilian woman also helped. I would not dissent from the commonly held view that Portuguese is the hardest of the Romance languages. On the world stage it is, nevertheless, an important tongue and worth having in one's linguistic quiver.

Because the Portuguese have been such inveterate travellers over the course of their history, Portuguese words have entered a number of languages. Vindaloo, a fiery Goan dish that is a staple of Indian restaurants, derives from the Portuguese for "garlic wine" since meat is marinated in this, and chilli, before cooking. The Portuguese were the first Europeans encountered by the Japanese and they left their mark on the Japanese language. The Japanese for bread is *pan* which comes from the Portuguese *pão*. Battered and deep-fried tempura was inspired by Portugal's fritter-cooking methods and is derived from *tempero*, the Portuguese word for seasoning.

From Chaves to Vila Pouca de Aguiar I had been following a road that is famous in Portugal, National Route 2. It runs from Chaves to Faro in the south and at 739 kilometres it's the longest road in the country. The Portuguese revere it as a kind of national monument, their answer to America's Route 66. It is a two-lane road, not too busy, that passes through a glorious variety of landscapes as it snakes its way to the Atlantic.

Without meaning any disrespect, I left National Route 2 at Vila Pouca de Aguiar and headed west through hilly country that immediately felt emptier. On one rather lonely stretch a vehicle with two officers from the Guarda Nacional Republicana, Portugal's gendarmerie, stopped beside me. The two officers talked courteously to me from inside their vehicle and offered me a lift. I graciously declined and they gave me a tip on where to camp for the night, an adventure park at a town called Santa Eulalia. It was one of those days marked by a dearth of cafés when the kilometres seemed very long, but I eventually reached the adventure park and put up my tent.

The next morning I walked through country which to my eyes was the loveliest I had seen since entering Portugal. To the north I enjoyed long vistas of green hills stretching out to the Spanish border. Also to the north, just below me in a valley half-hidden by roadside chestnut trees, was a quintessential Portuguese town, Ribeira de Pena. It's not famous but it looked picture perfect to me, with a twin-tower stone church at its centre, houses with red-tiled roofs and tidy fields on the town edge.

Then in the afternoon a sign told me that I was entering Vinho Verde country and vineyards cascaded down the hillsides. Soon the road crossed over the Tâmega River, more a big lazy brook than a torrent, with a shock of vibrantly green woodland bending over its waters. On days like this, drinking in the beauty, it feels just so perfect to be walking.

I was now in the historic province of Minho, a region that over the centuries provided many of the migrants who left the home country to make a new life in the colonies. This has been a land of small-holdings and big families where, according to the local saying, if a man put his cow out to graze in his own field the dung would fall on his neighbour's land.

I have long been fond of Vinho Verde, literally green wine, and it was a pleasure finally to be in the region where it is produced. Vinho Verde is young wine sold three to six months after the grapes are harvested. Fresh-tasting and slightly sparkling, it has to come from this designated region in the northwest of Portugal. It can be white, red or rosé, but most of the commercial production is white. In the town of Faia, journey's end for the day, I had the first chance to savour Vinho Verde in its native region. A glass cost all of 70 cents, but in the bar where I drank it proved difficult to spend even that. One of the male customers kindly insisted on treating me to two glasses and a plate of bread and ham. Faia didn't seem to go in for hotels and I spent the night in my tent again after a Brazilian woman allowed me to camp in front of her café.

One of my surprises in this initial phase of my walk was the striking presence of numerous modern wind turbines on the hilltops. After some nine days of actual walking in Portugal, I concluded that its government had a serious commitment to renewable energy. In country west of Faia, I was able to see, looking to my right, 25 turbines all turning in the breeze. A few metres further on, looking now to my left, I could see 36. By now I had seen countless hundreds of turbines.

On my fourth day of walking from Chaves I arrived in Fafe, home to the Museum of Migrations and Communities. This helped to fill out the story of Portuguese migration sketched out for me from one perspective by José and his wife Catherine. The museum is very modest in size and funding, but still it tells the visitor about two waves of emigration, the first to Brazil in the 19th and early 20th centuries and the second to France in the latter part of the 20th. Between 1836 and 1930 about 8000 people left Fafe for Brazil. The museum argues that the flow of migrants to Brazil had benefits for Portugal. Successful *brasileiros*, as they were called, pumped money back into their home country, acting either as philanthropists or industrialists.

According to the museum: "The best equipped schools, in terms of premises and teaching material, up to the Thirties in the centre and the north of the country were without a doubt those donated by 'brasileiros'."

The part of the museum devoted to France owes a lot to photos of Haiti-born painter and photographer Gérald Bloncourt who chronicled the lives of Portuguese immigrants living in Paris in the 1960s. His poignant black-and-white images give a sense of life on the edge – a small group of Portuguese migrants walking through mountains, a man having his hair cut while sitting on a chair outside in a shantytown in France. To this day there is a strong Portuguese community in France and you commonly hear the refrain that Paris is the third biggest Portuguese city, after Lisbon and Porto.

On this first stage of my journey, about halfway between Chaves and Fafe, I had a short, sharp experience of synchronicity. I fell to thinking about a travel book I admire, Paul Theroux's *The Old Patagonian Express*. I tried to remember the name of the Argentine literary giant whom Theroux met in Buenos Aires. The author in question, an Anglophile, recited the Lord's Prayer to Theroux in Anglo-Saxon. I walked and pondered and the name just didn't come. Then I turned a corner and to my left was a big sign with just one word – Borges. Of course, Jorge Luis Borges, essayist and poet. The solitary walker tends to have rather one-sided conversations with himself. When the external world chips in and makes a contribution, it comes as a bit of a shock.

CHAPTER 3

Birth of a Nation

The rivalry between Lisbon and Porto is legendary, but they are not the only Portuguese cities that love to hate one another – in a healthy way of course. Guimarães and Braga, the next two places of note on my itinerary, seem to have a similar dynamic to Lisbon and Porto. Sometimes a Braga native will readily admit that her city and Guimarães are ardent rivals. At other times what you get is a haughty curl of the lip and a refusal to admit that the good people of Braga waste any energy on Guimarães at all. In Braga, coarsely worded graffiti denouncing Guimarães tell their own tale.

I noticed the graffiti first and then observed another sign that perhaps these cities do not always warm to one another. They are only 21 kilometres apart, yet my map clearly shows that there is no rail link between them. Predictably enough, they are serious foes on the football field. One Braga native told me that the people of her city call residents of Guimarães Spaniards, while the Guimarães nickname for Braga folk is Moors. Neither epithet is meant to be at all complimentary.

Of course none of this affects the visitor in the slightest and both cities have much to offer. I walked into Guimarães first and checked into a hostel built in the mid-17th century. It was in one of the narrow, cobbled streets in the old part of the city. The hostel owner, Fausto Araújo, was a gentle, round-faced man with the air of a professor, steeped in the city's history. He told me first about his hostel, a granite structure with the biggest blocks of stone I have ever seen in a private building. He pointed out the heaviest stone, in the kitchen, which weighed six tonnes. Talk about the weight of history.

Soon in our conversation we were deep into the subject of the Napoleonic invasions of Portugal. Fausto said that in 1808 officers of the French army commanded by Marshal Soult insisted on being billeted in the best houses in Guimarães. Seven officers, he said, stayed in what is now his hostel. The natives, it turned out, were not at all friendly to the officers.

"When they stepped outside of the house after the first night they were ambushed and killed," said Fausto. "The same happened to most of the other officers. The army became headless – no officers."

Talking to Fausto, it felt as if the Napoleonic invasions of Portugal happened yesterday. He spoke with great disdain for the French armies and with warm admiration for the British military leader opposing them, Sir Arthur Wellesley, the future Duke of Wellington.

"They stole everything we had," he said of the French forces. "If you go to French museums they are full of Portuguese things."

The city's marketing pitch focuses on a period much further back, the 12th century, when Portugal first became an independent kingdom. On a tall building in central Guimarães the words "AQUI NASCEU PORTUGAL" (Portugal was born here) were lit up at night.

Guimarães' sense of identity and its tourist branding are entwined with Afonso Henriques, first king of an independent Portugal. Schoolchildren are brought in droves to Guimarães castle, where this giant in Portuguese history is said to have been born. The local football team, Vitória Sport Clube, depicts a very martial Afonso on its emblem, dressed for battle with drawn sword and shield. The club's home ground, as you've probably guessed, is the D. Afonso Henriques stadium.

There is a problem with this branding. Once upon a time, Portuguese historians all seemed to agree that the great man was born in Guimarães, but a highly charged academic debate shot this consensus to pieces in the 1990s. Now there are various views and the king's modern biographer, José Mattoso, favours the northern city of Viseu as royal birthplace.

In the end Afonso's birthplace is surely immaterial, but since he was such a central figure in the creation of Portugal let's take a look at him. Afonso was the son of Henri of Burgundy and Dona Teresa, natural daughter of King Alfonso VI of Léon and Castile. Different political visions drove Teresa and Afonso apart. A critical battle, with opposing forces led by mother and son, was fought near Guimarães, at São Mamede, in 1128. The son carried the day, defeating the soldiers of his mother and her Galician lover. His victory paved the way for Portugal's separation from the Kingdom of León, which covered the northwest part of the Iberian Peninsula. A victory by Teresa would have kept the little region of Portugal within the ambit of León.

One way and another, 1128 was a pivotal year in the invention of Portugal. The battle of São Mamede was not the only development. The arrival on the scene of a new Catholic military order also merits attention. It puts the creation of Portugal in the broader context of 12th century geopolitics, in particular the conflict between Christendom and the Muslim world. Bear in mind that we're talking of a period when Muslims ruled the whole southern half of Iberia.

At this point the story veers away to the prosperous Burgundian city of Troyes where in 1128 the Roman Catholic Church held an important council. One key participant in the council was

St Bernard of Clairvaux (1090-1153), a Burgundian abbot who through his work developing the Cistercian order became one of the most influential Europeans of his day. He also happened to be the uncle of Afonso. Bernard was an advocate of the Knights Templar, a newly formed group which at the Council of Troyes received official recognition as a Christian order. Also present at Troyes was Hugues de Paynes, a Burgundian who during a stay in Jerusalem a few years earlier had set up the Knights Templar to protect pilgrims to the holy city.

But what happened immediately after Troyes showed that there had been a shift in thinking. Hugues de Paynes and other members of the newly blessed Knights Templar did not make a beeline for Jerusalem; they went to Portugal. This is mainstream history. The Catholic Encyclopedia published in the early 20th century says Portugal was the first European country where the Templars settled, in 1128.

No one knows exactly who first had the idea of creating Portugal, but it seems that St Bernard backed the strategy of a new frontline state against the Muslim world. British author Martin Page, in his book *The First Global Village, How Portugal Changed the World,* quotes Burgundian chroniclers as saying that "the original intention was to create a new, model Christian nation on the western flank of Islam".

Certainly as the centuries unfolded, the histories of Portugal and the Knights Templar became profoundly intertwined. The whole nexus of relationships between Afonso on the one hand and the Knights Templar, Bernard's Cistercian order and Burgundy on the other did much to nurture the young state.

Afonso gave the Cistercians effective control over a great swathe of land north of Lisbon, known today as the Silver Coast. It extended from Obidos in the south to Leiria in the north. Into this region came Cistercian monks from Burgundy who brought modern farming methods, creating orchards and vineyards. They also organised boat building, fisheries and mining. Descendants of the Burgundian settlers who came to the area in the 12th and 13th centuries live there still. In the middle of this region, in the town of Alcobaça, Afonso put up the first Gothic buildings in Portugal, a Cistercian monastery meant as a gift for Bernard of Clairvaux.

Braga muscles in a bit on Portugal's creation story because its cathedral, the oldest in the country, has the tombs of Henri of Burgundy and Teresa. I toured Braga cathedral with a guide. Surveying the tombs in the Capela dos Reis, the guide said of Afonso: "If he had lost the battle, today we would all be hablando español."

Guimarães and Braga are such different places. My sense was that Braga is more sure of itself, not surprising given its size. It has a population of about 180,000 which makes it the third biggest city in Portugal. Guimarães has a population of about 68,000. While Lisbon and Porto, the two largest, now receive huge numbers of tourists, inland Braga is altogether quieter.

In the 20th century, there was one episode in Braga's history that the city does not highlight these days. It was in Braga in 1926 that Salazar gave a famous speech that set in motion a military coup, ushering in nearly a half-century of right-wing authoritarian government.

Braga's marketing pitch focuses on the great age of the city, founded by the Romans. The sign "BRACARA AUGUSTA CIDADE BIMILENAR" greets visitors. In other words Bracara Augusta, capital of the Roman province of Gallaecia, is 2000 years old.

But its crowning glory is medieval, the 11th century cathedral built before Portugal existed. Its treasures include a rusty iron cross said to have been used in the first Mass celebrated in Brazil in 1500. What caught my eye in the cathedral was a wall in the Capela da

Glória covered with 16th century Moorish-style geometric designs, alongside a Christian human figure. My guide in the cathedral said that whereas the Christian conquerors had expelled Moorish warriors after the Reconquista, artists and farmers of Muslim origin remained.

The cathedral is very much a working building. On one Saturday when I was in town a society wedding took place inside. There were the usual well-dressed women, with hats at crazy angles. A cream-and-black vintage car, a six-cylinder Humber Snipe, waited in front of the cathedral for the couple on their big day. Braga can definitely do style. A block or two away a busker, all verve and elbow, played the violin.

The city's main thoroughfare is the Avenida Central, a broad boulevard that was once elegant and is now faded. Tiles were missing on some of the buildings and the occasional roof had fallen in. Streets wax and wane and it would be idle to carp about this disrepair. What upset me was the presence of a two-storey McDonald's in a park area in the boulevard's central reservation. How could the authorities have decided that this was in keeping with the heart of one of Portugal's historic cities?

Most of the travellers I met in Braga were focused more on looking for work than on seeing the sights. I checked into a hostel and in the bed next to me was a gentleman named Wagner, a bearded barber from the Brazilian state of Parana. Wagner had scant interest in the rusty iron cross that might have been used in the first Mass in Brazil. The point of his adventures was to get work. He was travelling around Portugal, by train and bicycle, with all his hair-cutting equipment. He charged five euros a time for a haircut. One day he received a phone call offering him the position of trainee sushi-man in a Japanese restaurant in Lisbon. Within minutes, the bed next to me was empty. Wagner had gone, rushing to catch the first available train to the capital.

I made a more leisurely departure. From Braga I walked for three days through densely populated country to the wondrous city of Porto, which I made my home for six nights.

Porto guide Viriato in full flow

CHAPTER 4

A Storyteller in Porto

Every human settlement worth its salt needs storytellers and in Porto I was lucky to meet a master of the craft. On a wet November morning dozens of us gathered for a free English-language tour organised by Porto Walkers, a group of locals passionate about their city. I joined about 20 people from four continents who were guided by a Porto native called Viriato Morais.

Leading a walking tour of a major European city in the rain might daunt some, but Viriato delivered a virtuoso performance. He is a wiry, energetic man, a professional actor, born one day after Portugal's Carnation Revolution of 25 April 1974 that brought to a close nearly half a century of authoritarian rule. Our guide had one big thing helping him – the grandeur, the vitality of the historic Atlantic city that is Porto. After a period of stagnation in the 20th century it has now found its mojo again.

"Hello everyone, welcome to Porto. Welcome to Porto Walkers. My name is Vi... And who am I? Well, I am a local guy. I was born and raised in the city of Porto, although I have lived a little bit around the world. I lived in Spain, France, Belgium, England, Germany, Wales, Ireland, Scotland, Mexico, Angola, Brazil, well a little bit around the world. The main reason for that, it's because I am a professional actor."

Viriato, it transpired, had spent several months living in

Pembrokeshire and professed a love of Wales and the Welsh. More of that later, because the matter at hand right now is Porto. The first highlight of the tour was São Bento station, an unusual terminus in that tourists snapping pictures of its hand-painted tiles often seem to outnumber the train passengers. The tiles, about 20,000 of them, were the work of artist Jorge Colaço. The monumental task of painting and putting up the blue tiles, depicting scenes from Portuguese history, lasted from 1905 to 1916.

Viriato said of Colaço: "He was a Portuguese man, although he was born in Tangier, and he found a rule that came from the Moors that used to say that perfection belongs to God, so that way the artist or the creator cannot make a perfect job, otherwise he will be defying or insulting God." Viriato said the artist deliberately changed the position of five tiles, visible in the lower part of a battle scene, to avoid offending God.

Subjects tackled by Viriato ranged from art, architecture and history to the more edgy topic of consumer advice, offered as we stood on Porto's most important shopping thoroughfare, the 1.5-kilometre long Rua Santa Catarina. Our guide focused on one historic café on the street, with very fancy prices, and offered his take on marketing practice there.

"You're going to go inside and they will say 'Welcome, this is J.K. Rowling's table, welcome, this is J.K. Rowling's table, welcome, this is J.K. Rowling's table. Well, all the tables are going to be J.K. Rowling's table. And all of that because J.K. lived in Portugal between '91 and '94. But if you want to know a little bit more about her join the afternoon tour where that story will be developed in detail."

By speaking on a range of people and places with gusto and knowledge Viriato held everyone's attention, no mean feat for a tour of nearly three hours under grey skies and drizzle. We finished by walking down steep stone staircases to the quayside by the river

Douro, where Porto's priciest restaurants can be found. Viriato offered more consumer advice, useful for newcomers to Portugal. With total accuracy, he warned that many restaurants put bread, olives and other tidbits on the table when diners arrive. The unwary might think these are free, but they are not and can add significantly to the bill. "Send it all back if you don't want it," advised Viriato.

One message that came through strongly was that Porto's success in attracting tourists makes it very crowded in summer. Viriato said that in the past summer (2018) there were nine tourists for every inhabitant in Porto, about twice the comparable figure for Barcelona (4:1).

It was from Viriato's guided tour that I learnt what became my favourite Portuguese word. British expatriates living in the country are generally known for their inability to speak Portuguese. So they communicate often with a mixture of English and sign language. Viriato said that if the British wanted to convey that they had enjoyed the fish in a restaurant they would stick up a thumb and beaming broadly say "Fish". The Portuguese, bringing a sense of fun to the matter, now use the word "fish" to mean great or good. They have changed the spelling to "fixe" because that has the same sound as the English "fish". So, "O livro é muito fixe" means "The book is very good." The wonderful ways of language.

Viriato and I met again after the tour and we dug deeper into a few subjects. I said my understanding was that Porto had gone through a bad patch. Viriato concurred, saying that in the late 20th century "Porto, Portugal in general, with the wars, with our dictatorship, Porto was very much abandoned."

He then expanded on the very personal story of his birth, bringing together his country's political renewal and his arrival in the world. "I was born on the 26th of April 1974, so the very first day of democracy in this country. I spent the 25th trying to come out and on the 26th I was out. A struggle for freedom, just like my country."

When, I asked, did Porto hit bottom? "I would say the 80s. In the 80s Porto was a ghost town. Nothing was happening. I remember it was not safe at all to walk in the streets. Most of the neighbourhoods were not friendly... There was a big problem with drugs, drug addiction in Portugal, in the 80s and 90s."

He said the shift from dictatorship to democracy and the big exodus of Portuguese people from Africa when the colonies finally won their independence all contributed then to social tensions.

When we discussed the city's recovery, Viriato pinpointed 2001, when Porto was European Capital of Culture, as a turning point that ushered in years of transformation. "That was when you felt a massive change from the old city to the new city... Porto looked like a construction yard. We built the metro, we changed all the squares in the city."

Today Porto is bursting with tourists, many of them from Asia, and to illustrate the speed and scale of change Viriato told a story of something that happened in 1999. He had invited a Japanese friend to stay with him in Porto and one day the Japanese friend got lost and failed to appear for dinner. This was before mobile phones.

Viriato said: "I went to the main square and basically I screamed 'Anyone seen a Japanese?' And funnily enough a guy came out of a bar and said 'Yes, I saw one' and he pointed in this direction. So I went across the road and I screamed again and another came, 'I saw one.' ...He was the only Japanese guy in town." So the friend who was lost was found. "Can you imagine me asking that now in the city? That would be ridiculous today and we're talking about 19 years."

I asked Viriato if there was any downside to the tourism boom for the people of Porto. "There are loads of downsides, loads of downsides, but at the end of the day I still consider it positive," he said. One challenge now, with the crowded streets, was arriving on time for appointments. "Six years ago I could tell you 'I'll be there in 20 minutes' because those were the 20 minutes taken for the last 20 years…In the last six years, we don't know. It can take 20 minutes, it can take half an hour, 45 minutes, one hour because a lot of traffic, people in the streets, groups of tourists made it totally impossible to calculate that sort of time."

Another problem for locals has been steeply rising rents. "It is very difficult for the young generation to live in the city centre," he said, adding that a small studio apartment in the centre cost at least 600 euros a month while the minimum wage was 570 euros.

The city's population has haemorrhaged significantly in recent decades because of the poor living conditions in the late 20th century. Viriato said it had dropped from about 400,000 at the start of the 1980s to 216,000 today (2018). "Now people are trying to return to the city," he said.

He pinpointed the preservation of identity as the biggest struggle now faced by the people of Porto, which he said had historically been a "bubbling town" and a great trading centre with an independent spirit.

"What I felt in the last five years, when we started getting the revenues, the tourists started arriving, the big fight now for the people of Porto is really to keep their identity and to teach that to the people who will come and are coming to stay in Porto, because we have loads of foreigners who are coming to live in Porto nowadays.

"In the last five years the amount of people that came on vacation and decided at some point to actually move over, it's gigantic. So what we need – the obligation of the locals – is to pass that out to the people who are coming to stay in Porto. That passion that we have for the city, yes our roughness, our foul mouth, our 'heart in the throat' as we like to say, our not being afraid, but at the same time being family. So we are still very much a family here in town."

During the walking tour Viriato had said to me: "Wales is really my country. I am a Welshman inside." So when we met for our one-on-one conversation I asked him to say more. In his twenties he had spent at least six months in Wales, invited by a friend to the Pembrokeshire village of Llawhaden near Narberth. He did a range of things there, from decorating to teaching circus skills to local children.

What did he like about Wales? "Oh, wow, everything really. I have learned a lot in Wales, funnily enough. I was really lucky to be with amazing people, the community around there, all of them were amazing people, very friendly. They taught me a lot about farming, fishing, construction, beekeeping…"

"I felt that the Welsh were very similar to the Portuguese… We have loads in common, I would say, the Portuguese and the Welsh. We are the quiet ones. We are the cool ones, you know…Let us enjoy the good things in life."

On my last evening in Porto, I rather overdid the good things in life. I enjoyed too many glasses of Sangria and on my way to bed in my hostel slipped and fell on the stairs. I knocked myself unconscious and awoke in the arms of Igor from Kazan, one of my drinking pals in the hostel. He was most solicitous and so were the hostel staff. They called an ambulance and soon I was in a city hospital, having stitches sewn to mend a gash above my left eye.

In the morning I left the hospital under my own steam, collected my rucksack from the hostel and walked to the Douro with minutes to spare to catch a boat travelling upriver. I had already booked my place and paid my fare. With an ample bandage wound about my head, I must have cut a rather raffish figure. I felt very below par as I settled into the boat, but now all I had to do was sit back and watch the world go before.

CHAPTER 5

The Amazing Douro Valley

A while ago good friends from Canada crossed the Atlantic for a cruise on the Douro and that was the first time I realised the river was such an international draw. So I went to the Douro with high expectations and was very moved by what I found.

The Douro valley is truly extraordinary. It has breath-taking landscapes, including the steep terraced vineyards growing grapes for port wine, a rich history and an invigorating challenge to keep its best minds busy.

According to Jo Locke, Port and Portugal buyer for Britain's Wine Society, the Douro represents about half of the world's mountain viticulture. Just over 30,000 wine growers cultivate some 40,000 hectares, often working small parcels of land.

To do justice to the Douro, I departed from my usual rule on this Portuguese journey of walking from town to town. I covered some of the valley by foot, but I also travelled by boat and train. My idea was to get a more rounded experience of the river.

I began with a five-hour boat cruise from Porto to the town of Peso da Régua. The Douro is undoubtedly more scenic further upstream but the cruise was lazy, hazy travelling and I did learn that the Douro is not only about vineyards. At times forest clothed both riverbanks and I could fantasise about being in an unspoilt valley. But more often there were settlements in view, sometimes riverfront beaches with little boats, sometimes churches perched on a hill.

We day-trippers had a recorded commentary in Portuguese, English, French and Spanish so there was no missing the main elements of the story. One thing I learned was that the Douro used to have a coal-mining industry. On our right, not long after leaving Porto, we saw the relics of the Pejão coalfield closed by the Portuguese government in 1994 after more than a century of mining.

Closer to our destination and also on the southern bank, the commentary told us about a gentler activity – the growing of cherries around the town of Resende. Every year in May or early June the town hosts a two-day cherry festival and sells nearly five tonnes of the fruit to visitors. Locals say that their cherry harvest is the first of the year in Europe.

Our destination, Peso da Régua, has a special place in the valley's history. It was from here that the boats set out to Vila Nova de Gaia, opposite Porto, with barrels of wine to be stored and fortified to make port. The town has the excellent Douro Museum that tells the story of port wine and more besides. When I dropped by, the museum had an exhibition of highly evocative black-and-white photographs by Carlos Cardoso of the Douro's disused railway branch lines. But the main focus is wine and much of what follows I learned from the museum.

In the area that is now Portugal people were making wine well before the arrival of the Romans. In the Middle Ages wine production got a boost from Cistercian monasteries and some of the religious houses even had their own boats to get the wine to market.

The symbol of the Douro River is the *rabelo*, the traditional flat-bottomed boat perfect for negotiating the shallow waters of the river before the 20th century construction of dams. It was the *rabelos* that took the wine to Vila Nova de Gaia. The voyage downstream to the Atlantic coast took up to six days, while the journey home took on average a month and a half. The rabelos kept working until the 1960s. One *rabelo*, called Casa do Douro, stands on dry land in front of the museum.

It was, of course, the British in particular who developed a fondness for port. I don't know whether "moderation" was in Samuel Johnson's famous dictionary, but the word certainly didn't apply to his drinking habits. "I have drunk three bottles of port without being the worse for it," was his boastful comment on one occasion. In the 18th century drinking prodigious quantities of port just seemed to go with the territory of being an upper crust Brit.

The museum highlights several developments in that century that helped to establish the modern port industry. The first was the Methuen Treaty of 1703 between England and Portugal which made port wine and English woollens the basis of trade between the two countries. The treaty laid down that Portuguese wines imported into England would pay one third less duty than French ones.

Another was the decision by the man known to history as the Marquis de Pombal, chief minister and effective ruler of Portugal, to demarcate the boundaries of vineyards in the Douro valley. Pombal took this pioneering step in 1756, nearly a century before Bordeaux did the same sort of thing and he is hailed even today in the wine business as a visionary who established an AOC (*Appellation d'Origine Contrôlée*). Granite pillars, 335 in all and called *marcos pombalinos*, were set up to mark the wine region's limits. Pillar number one, erected in 1758, is on display in the Douro Museum.

The museum highlights the human sweat and toil that was central to the valley's development. It says: "Douro was one of the rare examples of capitalist agriculture in Portugal: between the late 18th century and the early 19th century over 30,000 Galician and

Portuguese labourers were busy building walls, pruning, grafting or harvesting, whether or not they had previous winegrowing experience." One museum guide told me that at least in northern Portugal the phrase "to work like a Galician" is still used today.

It happened gradually, but the British came to be a dominant force in the world of port. Just look at the big names in the commercial history of the drink – Symington, Sandeman, Dow, Graham, Taylor, Croft and Cockburn. Originally, all the Douro landowners were Portuguese and the British bought the wine from them and dealt with the export trade. But in the 19th century, when phylloxera infestations hit the Douro, British companies bought vineyard terraces at depressed prices, consolidating their position. Just under the surface, you can detect some local feeling in these parts about the strength of foreign business interests.

The international market for port is changing. France has become the world's biggest buyer of port, edging Britain into second place. Between 2006 and 2018 Portugal's port exports dipped by about 10 percent, but domestic consumption rose, apparently as a result of Portugal's tourism boom.

After a night's rest in Peso da Régua, I walked east on the road that follows the Douro upstream, on the southern side of the river. I was, finally, in the region where the port wine grapes grow. The famous terraced vineyards stretched up the hills, a beautiful golden brown. Night fell before I reached my destination, Pinhão, and a passing driver insisted on taking me the last few kilometres.

The small town of Pinhão is a favoured spot for tourist boats cruising the Douro to moor for a while. The town is on a bend in the river and on all sides vineyards reach for the sky. I wouldn't nominate Pinhão as the Best Portuguese High Street – it has too many shabby buildings. But the place does have a serenity, a quality of romance that embraces the Douro. I remember the scent of oranges ripening on the trees. I remember a brilliant moon.

For the full Douro experience, in Pinhão I boarded a train, for what has been hailed as one of the great little train rides of Europe. The train station in Pinhão puts you in a benevolent frame of mind before the journey even begins. It is decorated with winsome blue tiles showing traditional scenes from Douro life, such as women harvesting the grapes. The train follows the Douro as far as Pocinho, the eastern terminus of the line, which starts in Porto's São Bento station.

The charm of this one-hour ride was being so close to the river, on a stretch where there is no road. The ever-changing landscapes were a tonic for the eye. The classic terraced vineyards are there, of course, but the train also rattled past hillsides of bare rock, olive plantations, orange groves, posh houses and derelict buildings. The last time I had so enjoyed a train journey was about a quarter of a century earlier, travelling from the Chilean coast through the Andes to the Bolivian capital La Paz. After a coffee in Pocinho, it was back the same way to Pinhão. On both occasions there were few passengers, but it must be a different story in summer.

I wanted to talk to a winegrower and arranged to see Paulo Duarte, a small producer with a vineyard high above Pinhão in the village of Casal de Loivos. I didn't really know what to expect, but I confess that images of a nut-brown peasant bent over gnarled vines did spring into my mind. Predictably, the man I met was a suave confident businessman. During my visit he gave visitors a guided tour of his property in two foreign languages: English and French. Linguistic ability was just one part of his skill set. He also knew how to grow grapes and olives.

Two young polyglot women worked for him, serving the visitors with wine and chatting. The tourists tasted their wine on a terrace with magical views over the Douro valley and its vineyards.

A wine-tasting room with a view

Senhor Paulo, as everyone called him, talked to me after his visitors had gone. I said I had been walking through country regions where there was no one left under 60. How was it in his home valley? The Douro, he said, faced the identical problem – the young had gone.

"There are no people. The villages are deserted," said Paulo, adding that grapes were now mainly being harvested either by Portuguese from other regions or by foreigners from as far away as Romania.

In Vila Nova de Gaia, a few days earlier, I had gone on a port wine tasting tour and we had all watched a video about port. It showed local Portuguese women from the Douro picking grapes. After listening to Paulo, I felt that what we had seen was akin to a promotional video on London, showing men in bowler hats and rolled umbrellas. In other words, true of a certain era, but not an authentic depiction of today.

"The shortage of manpower is going to be a problem for us," said Paulo. "Is going to be a problem?" I asked, querying his use of the future tense. "It already is," he replied. I asked what he saw as solutions and he said that over the long term he foresaw greater mechanisation. Traditionally the Douro grapes have been picked by hand because the steep terraces make the use of machines impractical, but Paulo pinned his faith in new technologies, in smaller machines.

Right now, so during the 2018 season, lack of manpower, he said, had been one factor limiting his harvest and that of others in the valley. This had been a difficult year, partly because heavy rain in the summer had contributed to the spread of mildew in the grapes. He said his harvest had fallen by a third from the year before and he thought this was also the general experience in the Douro.

After this conversation with Paulo I went back to the Douro

Museum. A guide there told me that grape-pickers were now coming from as far away as Ukraine and Douro winegrowers had been obliged to put up their daily rates of pay to attract workers.

CHAPTER 6

Gifts from the Portuguese

From the Douro, a prime tourist destination, I headed south through less travelled country. The flavour was to be very different. The rationale for my route was that I wanted to pay my respects to the hometown of Aristides de Sousa Mendes, the Portuguese consul in Bordeaux who in 1940 helped thousands to flee Nazism by giving them visas in defiance of his government's orders. This meant a swing through country with few hostelries.

For me, the big themes on this eight-day journey from the Douro to Coimbra were the warmth and friendliness of people on my route and, yet again, the emptying of the countryside.

I set out from Peso da Régua on the Douro with no accommodation booked, trusting that at day's end I would find somewhere. Walking through country planted with vines I arrived first at the old cathedral city of Lamego. Following the advice of a local on the shortest route, I walked up all the monumental steps of the Sanctuary of Our Lady of Remédios, a shrine that took one-and-a-half centuries to build. Having climbed to the top, I then promptly lost my way. I found the right route eventually, but this episode rather shortened my walking day.

With nightfall approaching, I went into a bar in the village of Penude and asked the man serving whether he knew of anywhere to lodge in those parts. He said Father Adriano in the parish social centre next door would sort me out. I went there and got no further than the receptionist. I still had a bandage wrapped around my head, the legacy of my fall in Porto, and I think the receptionist instantly put me down as an undesirable. So there was no bed for me at the Catholic centre. The woman at the desk gave me the name of a restaurant a few kilometres further on and suggested I try there.

In steadily falling rain, I marched on. A woman on the other side of the road saw me, crossed over the road and thrust her umbrella into my hands. I was wearing waterproofs, top and bottom, but she felt this was not enough. A few days earlier another woman had stretched her arm out of a car window and given me a floppy hat. This sort of kindness is touching and I warmed to the Portuguese.

Still in the rain, a few kilometres further on, I spied another café and decided to make enquiries again. Now this is where the story of that evening started to get messy. But if the traveller omits all instances of messiness and puts out a narrative reeking of tidiness this distorts the truth. So I went into the second café and the woman serving said she knew a place where I could stay. She provided no details and insisted on treating me to a free soup. After my soup, since nothing seemed to be happening, I asked her where she had in mind for my lodgings. The parish social centre in Penude, said she. My heart sank and I explained that this establishment had already turned me away.

At this point another person stepped on stage into this little playlet. I'll call him Prizefighter. Now Prizefighter had been busy in the small bar making a nuisance of himself, going right up to other men and loudly spoiling for a fight. He now decided to take up metaphorical cudgels on my behalf. He phoned the priest whose social centre had sent me away. Although almost certainly drunk, Prizefighter was very well mannered in his conversation with Father Adriano. He appealed to the priest's humanity and Christian calling and painted a desperate picture of my plight. The priest held firm and Prizefighter conceded defeat. According to my benefactor's account of the conversation, Father Adriano said he had rooms for pilgrims walking north to Santiago de Compostela in Spain, but it was not his job to help unknown quantities heading south. Prizefighter was not finished yet. He phoned the restaurant a few kilometres ahead that might have rooms. He got a "no" from them too. With his job done, he bade us all goodnight and left.

Meanwhile it was still raining and night had fallen. There now followed a long conversation in the bar about my options. This ended with a man whom I'll call Driver telling me to jump in his car and we would head south prospecting for lodgings. Another man from the bar came too, so we were a proper little expedition.

We drove about 10 kilometres and Driver turned off the main road into a hamlet called Bigorne. He parked opposite a restaurant and in we went. One man stood alone in the restaurant and I put him down as the owner. Driver sketched out my plight, including the "no" from Father Adriano. The man listened carefully. Of generous girth, he had eyes that were both warm and shrewd. It became clear that he was not going to turn me away. Before he left, Driver told me that the man offering me a room was a Roman Catholic priest. His name was Father Agostinho Ramalho Pereira.

Soon I was seated at a family dinner, with Father Agostinho, his mother, his divorced sister Maria and her teenage daughter. Maria, it turned out, ran the restaurant next door, which explained Father Agostinho's presence there earlier.

We tucked into a saucepanful of boiled chestnuts. I was less nimble-fingered than my fellow diners and every now and then Father Agostinho would hand me a chestnut which he had extracted whole from its skin. I felt like an incompetent trainee.

We washed the chestnuts down with red wine from the Douro and then moved on to some chicken soup.

The conversation focused partly on pilgrimages and Father Agostinho said that many years earlier his mother and sister had walked the 200 kilometres to the shrine of Fátima in five days. An average of 40 kilometres per day! Since I had only occasionally managed 30 kilometres in a day I was shaken by this news. Portuguese pilgrims move in the fast lane. Mother and daughter had done the pilgrimage in May and on the first morning had set out at 6 a.m. Father Agostinho urged me to visit Fátima. I asked him whether he had been on the pilgrimage to Santiago de Compostela. He had, he said, adding with a twinkle: "By car." I enjoyed this family dinner after the fraught start to the evening. We spoke in Portuguese, but after dinner I discovered that Father Agostinho's niece spoke excellent English, learnt by watching interviews on YouTube.

After this enjoyable domestic interlude I hit the road again the next morning. When it came time to finding a bed, my experience was a neat counterpoint to the preceding day. In the village of Ribolhos, the woman who took care of the hostel for Santiago pilgrims didn't mind in the least that I was heading south. I took a bed in an otherwise empty hostel.

The next day, after nightfall, I walked into Viseu, the first major centre on my route since leaving the Douro. Viseu had a big city feel about it though strangely it had no train station. In Porto, the guide Viriato had said to me that Portugal was divided between Lisbon and "the border with Spain", meaning that the capital paid little attention to the rest of the country. Contemplating a city of about 100,000 people without a train station, it seemed that Viriato had a point.

I had one full day to see Viseu and it rained for much of that time. What do you do if you're in the middle of a strange city, it's raining and you're hungry? I think the answer to this question depends largely upon age. Being a pensioner, I got out my *Lonely Planet* guide to Portugal and discovered there was a recommended restaurant about 50 metres away. Doubtless a youngster would have whipped out a smartphone but the bookish approach works for me. So in no time at all I was out of the rain and inside a very cosy eatery called O Hilário, named for a 19th century fado singer born in the same street. My lunch hour inside the restaurant reminded me of one great gift from the Portuguese – they listen. Admittedly I was the only customer, but the man who served me told me about the fado singer and about his city and listened to what I had to say. The conversation was food for thought.

In 2017, close to 13 million foreign tourists spent holidays in Portugal and the tourism sector is now the country's biggest employer. The country has great beaches, including the world's highest surf, historic cities and reasonable prices. But I think one factor in this success story is what I found in O Hilário – the readiness to listen and to talk. I don't know why the Portuguese are such good listeners, but they are.

Well restored by lunch, I made for Viseu's Grão Vasco Museum, which has paintings by one of Portugal's leading Renaissance artists, Vasco Fernandes (c.1475-1542). Known as Grão Vasco (the Great Vasco), he made his reputation with art works for Viseu cathedral, which stands next door. What gripped my attention was a painting with a different spin on the familiar theme of the Three Wise Men visiting the baby Jesus. Balthazar, sometimes depicted as a Black man, in this painting is shown as a Brazilian Indian with a feather headdress and a spear. The museum says this painting, done soon after the Portuguese "discovery" of Brazil in 1500, is the first depiction of an Indian from the Americas in Western art. It is striking that in his very first appearance the indigenous American is thrust into the central narrative of Christianity.

Some poignant artwork in Parada de Gonta

From Viseu to Coimbra was a three-day walk, still off the beaten track. I hiked through country where some of the villages had been so sapped by emigration that they seemed to be holding on by their fingernails. In one village south of Viseu, Parada de Gonta, where there were derelict buildings in the centre, on Emigrant Avenue an artist had painted a simple blue tile decoration showing two couples with suitcases and boxes heading for a train. I found it very poignant.

I finally reached the old mansion of Aristides de Sousa Mendes, in the town of Cabanas de Viriato. It stood out in a sprawling residential district, amidst big houses and gardens with well-laden orange trees. There were plans to turn the house into a memorial museum about his life and achievements in sparing Jews and others from Nazi death camps. The website sousamendesfoundation.org said the restoration was well under way, helped by a grant from the European Union.

It was perhaps eccentric of me to traipse through the Portuguese countryside to see this place, which was not yet open to the public. I learned from my visit that a statue of another rebel stands in the hometown of Sousa Mendes, that of Viriato, the most important leader of the Lusitanians resisting the Romans in the second century BC. There seems to be a bit of rebel DNA in these parts.

CHAPTER 7

Thoughts on the Portuguese Empire

My encounter in Viseu with the first American Indian in Western art turned my thoughts towards the Portuguese Empire. This overseas dimension of Portugal's history has been so much part of the country's essence that I have decided to give a brief account of the empire or else these won't be adequate reflections.

Portugal's feverish burst of energy in the 15th and 16th centuries is one of the remarkable pioneering endeavours in history. It was a tale of superhuman drive and courage that saw a small European nation create a seaborne empire that stretched from Brazil to Africa and on to the East Indies. It was also a story of desperate cruelty. The Portuguese embodied utter ferocity and from Mombasa in Africa to Goa and Malacca in the East they sacked Muslim trading hubs and slaughtered the inhabitants.

The Portuguese were the pathfinders, the first Europeans to sail into the wider world beyond the Mediterranean and the Atlantic and gain direct access to the riches of the East. They showed great bravery and skill and played a central role in the scientific task of mapping the world. At the same time they murdered and stole and enslaved, setting the tone for a ruthless European dominance of the globe.

In the words of British historian J.H. Plumb: "The Portuguese made the breach through which the jackals raced to get their fill."

The creation of this empire raises so many questions. What impelled the Portuguese to set out on unknown seas and maintain this global string of dominions? Given that the Portuguese population was only between one million and 1.5 million souls, how on Earth did they do it? What values did they take with them? Why did the empire fade? What is its legacy?

In his classic work *The Portuguese Seaborne Empire 1415-1825,* British historian C.R. Boxer gave four main motives for Portugal's global expansion: "(i) crusading zeal against the Muslims, (ii) the desire for Guinea gold, (iii) the quest for Prester John, (iv) the search for Oriental spices." (Prester John was a legendary Christian priest-king in Africa.)

A pithier summary comes from a famous conversation between a crew member on Vasco da Gama's first voyage to India and two Spanish-speaking Tunisians in Calicut. "What the devil has brought you here?" they asked. "We have come to seek Christians and spices," came the reply.

As the Portuguese built settlements away from their continental home, they knew they were creating a new narrative, birthing a New World. Boxer writes that on Madeira, which the Portuguese began to settle in the 1420s, the first boy and girl born were christened Adam and Eve.

For Portugal, much was propitious and set the scene for extraordinary expansion. In 15th century Europe, Portugal was exceptional in not being convulsed by war. This internal peace provided the necessary backdrop for empire-building. The country was poor. Ill-distributed rain, inferior soil, over-population, plague – these were some of the factors that drove individual Portuguese to seek their fortunes overseas. Outbreaks of plague ravaged Portugal in the 16th and 17th centuries, whereas Brazil, until yellow fever hit in the 1680s, must have seemed a healthier option.

Gold can draw men on and in the history of Portugal's empire the yellow metal made its appearance in two distinct narratives. The Guinea gold was the fabled gold of West Africa, from the Upper Niger and Senegal rivers. The Portuguese never succeeded in finding these elusive inland gold workings, but their gold trade with Africa started early. According to Boxer, the Portuguese first obtained African gold dust through barter with Touaregs in 1442. It seems that soon gold was flowing in quantity into Portugal because in 1457 the Lisbon mint resumed issue of gold coinage, with the *Cruzado* (Crusade). Portugal had had no gold currency of its own since 1383. Much later, at the end of the 17th century, began the Brazilian gold rush, the first and longest of modern times.

After this quick look at why, let's move on to how. Portugal, with its tiny population, faced the challenge of how to man its ships and fight its wars. Before modern medicine, maritime empires devoured human lives on a terrifying scale. The passage from Portugal to India took six to eight months and the mortality rate could be very high, with dysentery, typhus and scurvy all taking their toll. In a fleet that went to India in 1571, nearly 2,000 men died out of the 4,000 who sailed from Lisbon.

There was a light-hearted side to Portugal's shortage of skilled manpower. The chronicler Castanheda recounted a story about one ship that set sail for India in 1505 with a raw crew. These brand-new mariners could not tell port from starboard when their ship left the Tagus. The captain found a solution, tying onions on one side of the vessel and garlic on the other. "Now," he instructed the pilot, "tell them to onion their helm or to garlic their helm and they will understand quick enough."

But there was a dark side too. Portugal solved the manpower problem, as did other seafaring nations, by using force or legal diktat – think of Britain's press gangs. Portuguese courts sentenced petty thieves and offenders to exile. These exiles were called *degredados*.

There were *degredados* on the pioneer fleets of Vasco da Gama, and Boxer says every fleet that left Lisbon for the colonies in the 17th and 18th centuries had its quota of them. Simply belonging to the wrong ethnic group could also be a ticket to the colonies. The 18th century monarch John V forcibly exiled entire Roma communities to Brazil and Angola, with no formal charge being laid against them.

In their armies, the Portuguese overcame the manpower shortage by making more use of African slaves than any other European country. Portugal's rivals acknowledged the slaves' fighting qualities. In 1622 the Dutch attempted to seize Macao from Portugal, but failed.

"The Portuguese beat us off from Macao with their slaves," according to one contemporary Dutch account. "It was not done with any soldiers, for there are none in Macao…"

Another tactic was to recruit boys. According to Boxer, soldiers of 12, 10 or eight years were reasonably common. By fair means and foul, Portugal put together armies that in the 16th century fought campaigns from the interior of Mozambique to the island of Ceylon.

Men alone do not build an empire; there is also the matter of technology. At the start of its expansion, Portugal's shipbuilding prowess was second to none. Its lateen-rigged caravels, light-weight craft with triangular sails, were able to sail closer to the wind than any other European vessel.

The diplomatic green light for Portugal's imperial success was the historic treaty of Tordesillas, concluded between Portugal and Castile in the remote Spanish town of that name in 1494. This treaty basically carved up the world outside Europe between the two kingdoms. It created a north-south dividing line that ran 370 leagues (1,184 nautical miles) west of the Cape Verde islands. Everything to the east of this would belong to Portugal, while all lands to the west would be Spanish.

This extraordinary agreement has been hailed as one of the greatest coups in diplomatic history. Little Portugal won the right to the great chunk of South America which became known as Brazil. In 1494, the mainland of America had not officially been discovered by Europeans. But there has been consistent speculation that the Portuguese knew perfectly well it was there and waited until 1500 before announcing that they had "discovered" Brazil.

The values the Portuguese brought to empire-building were inevitably those of the Europe of their day. Their methods were brutal and all the European nations who followed them as colonisers included inhumanity in their lexicon. Vasco da Gama set the tone. Chronicler Gaspar Correia recounts that he ordered his men to cut off the hands, ears and noses of prisoners and he then sent them to a local Indian ruler with the suggestion that these human scraps be made into a curry. On one occasion the Portuguese icon sank a ship with 200 Muslim pilgrims. Revered in Portugal, Vasco da Gama does not enjoy the same high esteem in Asia.

At stake in the East Indies was the lucrative spice trade and for all the main players in the game, war was the ultimate arbiter. When the Portuguese first sailed into Asian waters, they found no serious naval rivals. Egypt, Persia and the empire of Vijayanagara in South India had no warships in the Indian Ocean. But this state of affairs did not last long. The Portuguese threatened Venice's spice trade with the east, through the Red Sea and the Gulf, and made an enemy of the republic.

The Venetian Republic joined a mainly Muslim alliance to try to crush the nascent Portuguese empire out east. Venice sent war galleys and carracks to Alexandria where its shipwrights helped to disassemble them and then reconstruct them on the Gulf of Suez. This epic undertaking was the prelude to the Battle of Diu, fought off the northwest coast of India in 1509 between the Portuguese and this intercontinental coalition, which included the Ottoman Empire. The Portuguese won the day in one of the decisive naval battles of history. After it, they were the lords of the Indian Ocean and centuries of European dominion of these waters then followed.

The most energetic embodiment of Portuguese imperial values in the early 16th century was Afonso de Albuquerque, a tall larger than life character with a beard that grew down to his waist. Albuquerque (1453-1515) was a hurricane of a warrior, the "Caesar of the East" who became the Governor of Portuguese India. He built a reputation for military brilliance, ferocity and broad vision. In a fight at Calicut, Albuquerque received arrows to the throat and arm and a bullet to the chest but he shrugged off his wounds and survived. One of his great ambitions was to capture the Prophet Mohammed's tomb from Mecca.

Albuquerque led the Portuguese in the capture of Goa in 1510 and the conquest of Malacca the following year. After the sack of Goa, Albuquerque wrote to King Manuel: "I have burned the town and killed everyone…We have estimated the number of dead Muslim men and women at six thousand. It was, sire, a very fine deed."

There is a contrast between the behaviour of the first Europeans into Asian waters and the comportment of the Chinese in the great fleets of Admiral Zheng He. Between 1405 and 1433 these fleets visited Southeast Asia, India, Arabia and East Africa. Although his ships carried soldiers, Zheng, born into a Muslim family, on the whole used force sparingly.

For the Portuguese, hatred of Islam and material greed went hand in hand. The scale of the greed is clear from the sad tale of Albuquerque's flagship, the *Flor de la Mar*. This ship was overloaded with treasure, including four golden statues of lions, looted from the Sultan of Malacca's palace. But in late 1511 the *Flor de la Mar,* with Albuquerque on board, was wrecked off Sumatra. Albuquerque and some of his crew were rescued but the ship perished. No one really knows whether this fabulous treasure was salvaged by locals or survivors, or whether it lies there still after more than five centuries.

It was not part of the 16th century European mindset to tolerate other religions and the Portuguese acted in accordance with European attitudes prevailing in their day. From a 21st century vantage point, however, their actions still have the power to shock. Boxer tells us that the Archbishop of Goa publicly pounded to bits in a mortar and pestle the sacred relic of Buddha's tooth captured in Ceylon. In Goa in 1540, the Portuguese embarked on the mass destruction of Hindu temples. A series of laws were enacted for Portuguese-controlled territory with the aim of preventing public worship for Hindus, Muslims and Buddhists. The Portuguese built churches on the sites of destroyed mosques and temples and transferred income from these properties to the Roman Catholic Church. Ritual bathing, such a big feature of Hinduism, was banned.

Portugal changed the religious map of Asia, sometimes achieving mass conversions to Christianity. Tens of thousands of Parava pearl-fishers, in conflict with Muslims over fishing grounds in southern India, became Christian. St Francis Xavier (1506-1552), born in present-day Spain, was the central figure in this endeavour. He was also a pioneer missionary in Japan, where the Portuguese arrived before any other Europeans.

Even the briefest reflections on the empire have to focus on Portugal's role in slaving. The chronicler Gomes Eanes de Zurara has provided a poignant vignette from the beginnings of the Portuguese slave trade. He describes Prince Henry the Navigator, mounted on a horse, watching the arrival on 8 August 1444 of 235 slaves in Lagos bay in southern Portugal.

The chronicler wrote: "What heart, however hard, could fail but to be stung at the sight of such an event?"

This was probably the first major arrival of slaves in Europe.

The trade grew to be enormous and the Portuguese became the biggest slavers in the world. According to data collected by Emory University in Atlanta, Georgia, Portuguese vessels carried about 5.8 million slaves across the Atlantic between the early 16th and late 19th centuries. Britain was the second biggest slaving nation.

But whereas cities like Liverpool, London and Bordeaux have museums recording their roles in the history of slavery, Lisbon has nothing. Historians and journalists have faced a struggle to get acknowledgement of the dark side of Portugal's empire. Boxer was for a while banned from Portugal by the dictator Salazar because he did not adhere to the official narrative of a benign Portuguese dominion. Barry Hatton, in his book *The Portuguese,* pays tribute to the Portuguese journalist Ana Barradas who in her 1991 *Black Book of the Portuguese Discoveries* sought to draw attention to the violence that often marked Portuguese rule. "Her book, however, is hard to find," notes Hatton ruefully.

In the days of slavery very few Portuguese raised their voices against the trade. One critic was Father Fernando Oliveira, author of the first printed Portuguese grammar. In a book on naval warfare, published in 1555, he dedicated a chapter to a rejection of the slave trade. According to Boxer, after that came two hundred years of Portuguese silence on the subject.

(In the years immediately after my long walk, the whole question of the trans-Atlantic slave trade and its relevance to current race relations moved strongly up the international agenda. In March 2021, Europe's leading human rights group, the Council of Europe, rebuked Portugal for not doing enough to confront its slaving past.

"Further efforts are necessary for Portugal to come to terms with past human rights violations to tackle racist biases against people of African descent inherited from a colonial past and historical slave trade," the Council said in its annual report on Portugal.

The Council also called on the Lisbon government to rethink how schools teach the country's colonial past, which is usually seen as a matter of pride. Schools teach little about Portugal's huge role in the slave trade.)

Historical analysis of race relations in Portugal's empire has undergone a radical shift over the past half-century. There was once a view, propagated by the 20th century Brazilian sociologist Gilberto Freyre, that Portuguese colonial authorities fostered the social ascent of Black men. It was Boxer who led the charge in demolishing that claim. He writes that throughout the colonial period in Brazil a rigid colour bar operated, excluding full-blooded Black men from municipal office-holding.

Being a Jew was for centuries potentially dangerous in Portuguese domains. The Portuguese Inquisition, from 1591 onwards, sent commissioners on visits to Brazil, partly to seek out ethnic Jews suspected of practising Judaism in secret. When the Dutch occupied Recife, from 1630 to 1654, some Jews openly practised their religion. But when the Portuguese returned, these Jews thought it prudent to leave Brazil and they helped to found the Jewish community in New York.

All empires exploit – it's what they do. So the civilisations and the ecosystems that they encounter predictably feel the friction of their passage. Since the Portuguese were the trailblazers, they were the first Europeans to impact the ecosystems of Asia and sub-Saharan Africa.   Teak forests on the western coast of India fell to their axes, for the shipwrights of Goa to build boats. Detective work by a multi-disciplinary team of scientists has shed light on the Portuguese role in the thinning of Africa's elephant populations. In 2008, men looking for diamonds off the coast of Namibia found the wreck of the *Bom Jesus* which sank on a voyage to India in 1533. Alongside hundreds of gold coins were more than 100 elephant tusks, well preserved in the cold waters of the Atlantic.

Researchers discovered that the tusks came from 17 unrelated elephant herds. Only four of these herds are known to exist today, so we are now better informed on the scale of the destruction.

The decline of Portugal's empire sprang largely from the cold, hard logic of European demographics. Portugal was one small corner of an increasingly dynamic, thrusting continent. But Portugal itself contributed to the process of decline. In the 16th century, one man made a catastrophic decision. That man was King Sebastian who at the age of 24 took it into his head to spread Christianity by the sword in Morocco. Now Portugal began its empire in Morocco, when it captured the town of Ceuta in 1415. But Sebastian wanted more and a shambles of a crusade lurched off to Africa. In scorching summer heat in 1578, against the advice of his commanders, Portugal's king insisted on taking his army into the Moroccan interior. He then led the flower of his country's nobility to its doom at the Battle of El-Ksar el-Kebir. Historian A.R. Disney evokes the scene. He writes that Sebastian, in full body armour under the African sun, rode to his death with men pouring water over him to keep him cool.

Portugal laid no blame on Sebastian for this disaster. Out of the battle grew the superstition that the king was not really dead – no survivors admitted to having seen him killed. The legend arose that one day Sebastian would return and lead Portugal to a great and glorious future. This belief, called Sebastianism, was for a long time a shaping ideological force among the Portuguese. Sebastianism fostered the mentality that all one had to do was to wait for the saviour. It took various forms; depending on whom you listened to, Sebastian was biding his time in a cave or on a misty Atlantic island. It survived in the backlands of Brazil, in modified versions, until the twentieth century.

After this tragedy in Morocco, Portuguese independence also died – for three generations. King Philip II of Spain used an invasion force, backed by bribes of silver to leading Portuguese, to bring the weakened kingdom into a dynastic union with Spain. Portugal's "Sixty Years of Captivity" under Spanish rule began in 1580. Catholic Spain at this point faced the revolt of its Protestant Dutch subjects, so Portugal was sucked into this titanic struggle. The Dutch began to go on the offensive against Portuguese possessions in the late 1590s, in West Africa.

This was the prelude to a dismal century for Portugal's standing. Its rivals, sometimes acting together, began to chip away at its dominions. The Persians, with naval support from the English, wrested Ormuz from Portugal in 1622. But it was the Dutch who did the gravest damage. Their attacks played a big role in convincing the Portuguese that they should break away from Spain. The Portuguese revolt against Spain, which began in 1640, in fact brought no relief from the attentions of the Dutch. Portugal found itself fighting an independence war against the Spanish and a colonial war against the Dutch at the same time.

Boxer argues that the 17th century struggle between Spain and Portugal on the one hand and the Netherlands on the other deserves to be called the First World War. He captures the vast geographical spread of this war and the high stakes.

"Apart from Flanders fields and the North Sea, battle was joined in such remote regions as the estuary of the Amazon, the hinterland of Angola, the island of Timor and the coast of Chile. The prizes included the cloves and nutmegs of the Moluccas; the cinnamon of Ceylon; the pepper of Malabar; silver from Mexico, Peru and Japan; gold from Guinea and Monomotapa; the sugar of Brazil and the Negro slaves of West Africa."

The outcome for Portugal of the "First World War" was victory in Brazil, stalemate in Africa and defeat in Asia. Dutch victory over Portugal was down to their stronger economy, more sea power and more manpower – they made much use of Germans and Scandinavians in their forces.

One thread in Portugal's decline was its decision to cut itself off from the mainstream of European intellectual life. From about 1550 Portugal operated a system of triple censorship. No book could be published unless approved by the High Court of Justice, the local bishop and the Portuguese Inquisition. Imports of books were strictly controlled. This totalitarian system was in force for nearly three centuries and the ideas of the Scientific Revolution, much discussed elsewhere in Europe, had no hearing in Portugal. Portugal's Jesuits forbade discussion of the works of Newton, Descartes, Leibnitz, Bacon, Hobbes and other leading thinkers.

Nor did the Portuguese maintain their lead in the area of navigational knowledge. Dutchman Jan Huyghen van Linschoten, who had served as the archbishop's secretary in Goa in the 1580s, carefully copied Portugal's secrets and published a work with detailed charts of the East Indies and critical nautical data such as currents. The Portuguese, having once been the leaders in navigational expertise, dropped to the rear.

Despite its string of defeats in the 17th century, and then Brazilian independence in the 19th century, Portugal clung on to substantial colonies until the second half of the 20th century. While other European governments bowed to the winds of change in sub-Saharan Africa, Portugal fought on, surrendering its colonies of Guinea-Bissau, Mozambique and Angola only after long bloody wars. Even for little Goa, in Asia, it put up a fight. In 1961, India launched attacks by land, sea and air to capture the island that had been Portuguese for 451 years.

The African wars, which grew to be deeply unpopular, had a convulsive effect on society. They led to the military coup in 1974 that ended nearly half a century of authoritarian rule and established democracy. The new government promised independence to the African colonies and, in one of the significant migrations of modern times, more than half a million Portuguese settlers in Africa chose to return to the mother country.

What is one to make of all this Portuguese sound and fury that echoed around the world for centuries? It cannot be dismissed as signifying nothing, but it's hard to take a definitive stance on legacy – every generation will probably take its own view on how to assess this history.

On the credit side, one important thing that Portugal took to the wider world was clearly the Portuguese language. It is remarkable that this language, mother tongue of a small nation in the northern hemisphere, is now the most important in the global south. Portuguese is spoken by more people than French or German. With about 220 million native speakers, Portuguese is usually ranked as the world's sixth most widely spoken language. Most of the native speakers are in what used to be Portuguese colonies – Brazil, five African countries and East Timor in the Far East. It has fallen to the Brazilian city of São Paulo to host the Museum of the Portuguese Language. The museum is housed in the Luz train station, a venue full of symbolism because this was the arrival point for many immigrants meeting the Portuguese language for the first time.

São Paulo, as it happens, also weighs in with a reminder of the debit side of the equation. It has the Latin America Memorial, which opened in 1989 as a monument to the integration of the region. At the memorial, designed by Brazilian architect Oscar Niemeyer, is a sculpture representing a left hand bleeding, so stained with red. The inspiration for the sculpture came from the book *Open Veins of Latin America: Five Centuries of the Pillage of the Continent.* This 1971 book was the work of Eduardo Hughes Galeano, a Uruguayan writer with Welsh blood in his veins. It chronicles the suffering of a continent under colonial rule and it has helped to shape how Latin

Americans view their history. That painful history lies beyond the scope of this book.

In the end, perhaps what stands out above all else is that the Portuguese helped to create a new chapter in human history. When they rounded the southern tip of Africa, they wove connecting threads for the One World story where we are now all interconnected.

The first European to sail into the Indian Ocean was Portugal's Bartholomeu Dias in 1488. He gave inspired leadership to the small flotilla he led down the west coast of Africa, turning away from the shore and out into the Atlantic hoping to harness westerly winds. Roger Crowley, in his book *Conquerors: How Portugal Forged the First Global Empire,* hails Dias's decision to head into the open Atlantic as "a decisive moment in the history of the world". During this voyage, Dias's ships were within the limits of the southern iceberg zone.

Vasco da Gama's voyage to India a decade later, in terms of organisation, seamanship and endurance, was a marvel. The voyage was meticulously planned, the crew was well paid and there were Arabic speakers in the fleet. While Christopher Colombus looms large in the popular imagination, his crossing of the Atlantic in 1492 was a lesser feat than the achievements of the Portuguese explorers. Colombus took 71 days to sail the 4,000 miles to the Bahamas. Da Gama sailed 12,000 miles from Lisbon to Calicut in India and it took him 309 days, 93 of them out of sight of land. This was a 15th century moonshot.

CHAPTER 8

The First Capital of Portugal

It is quite a while since Coimbra was the capital of Portugal – 763 years before my visit, to be exact. But the visitor quickly picks up that this city, in its bones, still doesn't like playing second fiddle to anyone. Coimbra was the country's first capital, from 1131 to 1255, and memories in Portugal are long.

I experienced Coimbra as deeply feminine, like a Portuguese woman singing fado, soulful, sensual and rich in feeling. Seen from the other side of the Mondego River, with its golden buildings reflected in the waters, the city looked to me like a painting by Claude Monet, with flow and colour and poetry.

I learned a new tongue twister when visiting this city – Conimbricense, meaning a native of Coimbra. The Conimbricenses are proud of their city. Its narrow winding backstreets feel just like an old human settlement should. Coimbra is home to the oldest university in the Portuguese-speaking world. It is the burial place of the country's first two kings. It has been the cradle of much Portuguese art, in particular sculpture. It was the scene of Portugal's most famous love story and its bloody end.

Like all of Portugal's big cities, Coimbra was a major centre in Roman times. Its Machado de Castro National Museum is remarkable. The museum is built on top of the Roman forum that had to be supported by a complex cryptoportico of vaulting that enabled the forum to be flat on a hilly site. Visitors can walk through these profoundly atmospheric Roman galleries and that is an experience I have never had in any other museum.

One distinctive feature of the city is the architectural echo of the 350 years, from 714 to 1064, when the Moors ruled the city. This eastern influence is part of its charm and a reminder of the period when the lands that now form Portugal belonged to the Muslim world. Coimbra's Arco de Almedina looks so very Middle Eastern that it is easy to imagine a camel appearing at any moment to pass through the gate.

One day in November, strolling through the centre of Coimbra past expensive shops, I saw several posters recalling a very different age and culture. In a street clearly dedicated to consumerism were images of Lenin in jacket and tie, with right arm outstretched, addressing a Russian crowd. A hammer and sickle and the letters PCP showed the posters were the work of the Portuguese Communist Party and they were inviting the good people of Coimbra to a dinner to celebrate the October Revolution of 1917. Posters of Lenin are not common in 21st century Europe and rather catch the eye. They were a reminder that the Communist Party is still a force in Portuguese politics, though not as powerful as it once was in the late 20th century.

A big part of Coimbra's sense of identity comes from its university which has had a curious history. It began life in Lisbon in 1290 and then shuttled back and forth between Lisbon and Coimbra before settling permanently in Coimbra in 1537. Today there is a highly cosmopolitan student body and students are a conspicuous element in city life.

The jewel in the university's crown is arguably the Biblioteca Joanina, a remarkable 18th century Baroque library. The visitor enters the building on a floor below the books library and is directed first into prison cells where miscreant students were incarcerated. The university had its own legal system, but after a liberal revolution in Portugal in 1834 the prison cells were used to store books. A visit to the cells was a surreal, unexpected prelude to seeing the library, a magnificent structure with frescoed ceilings. The university is very proud of the library's resident colony of bats, which eat the insects that would otherwise devour the books. Apparently, there is only one other library in the world with resident bats and that is the Mafra Palace Library, also in Portugal.

One day I crossed the Mondego River and went to a place called the Quinta das Lagrimas (Estate of Tears), associated with the most celebrated love story in Portuguese history and its gruesome end. Today, rather incongruously, you walk past a golf academy to reach the place where, according to legend, noblewoman Inês de Castro was murdered in 1355. The estate is said to be haunted by her ghost. King Afonso IV ordered the murder because he disapproved of his son Peter's romance with her. Three assassins stabbed Inês to death and then decapitated her. After Peter became king two years later, he ordered that the killers' hearts be torn from their bodies. Operas, ballets, poems and plays have immortalised the tale, still known to every Portuguese. Peter and Inês are buried in two great Gothic tombs in northern Portugal's Alcobaça monastery, the one built by King Afonso Henriques in the mid-12th century as a gift to Bernard of Clairvaux.

I tried to explore one broad social question connected with Coimbra's history, namely what happened to all the Muslims when Moorish rule came to an end in 1064. I contacted Coimbra's small modern mosque in a northern suburb and arranged to go and see members of the Muslim community. When I turned up I was kindly invited into Friday afternoon prayers. A teenage boy from Turkey, using sign language, gave me instructions on the necessary ablutions prior to entering the prayer room. It was the first time

I had been admitted to a Muslim service. About 40 worshippers, all male, were in attendance.

After prayers I talked to the mosque's long-serving imam, Mamadou Saidou Diallo, from Guinea. "What happened to all the Muslims in Coimbra after the Reconquista?" I asked. "I think they were all expelled, but I am not sure," he said. Today's Muslim community in Coimbra, he said, was about 100 strong and included people from the Indian sub-continent, the Middle East and Africa.

There are comments in the Old Cathedral of Coimbra which suggest that some Muslims remained. At the tomb of Sesnaldo Davides, the first governor of Coimbra after the Reconquista, there is a modern tribute to him. It reads: "With rare qualities as a diplomat and with a great capacity for dialogue, Sesnaldo established peace and respect between the Christian and Muslim communities of the region."

Portugal's long Reconquista of lands from the Moors carried on until 1249 when the last enclave, Faro in the Algarve, was finally taken.

In the words of historian A.R. Disney: "A grand experiment in inter-communal existence on European soil had finally ended in failure."

CHAPTER 9

Overload at Fátima

I set off from Coimbra on a misty morning, crossing a bridge over the Mondego as cormorants swarmed over the waters just downstream. Right from the centre of Coimbra there were waymarks for Fátima, Portugal's leading shrine. This was the first time on my Portugal journey I had followed a waymarked route. It is a subtly different kind of journey – there is a feeling of being held somehow, of being part of an invisible flow of pilgrims who have gone before. Fátima waymarks are blue. For the first couple of hours or so, to a village called Cernache, there was a blue strip on the minor road I was following every 12 paces or so.

Later the pilgrims' way went right past the ruined walls of Conímbriga, one of the biggest Roman settlements excavated in Portugal. Finally, in the afternoon, the waymarked route became a footpath wending its way through some gorgeous countryside, with wooded ravines and then a little brook running parallel to the path. What a joy to leave roads behind! One feature of the day was farmers harvesting olives in the traditional manner. With blankets laid on the ground for women to collect the olives, men typically climb the trees and shake the branches.

After spending the night in a hostel in the town of Rabaçal I hit the trail again. Shortly before nine o'clock guns started popping. It was a hunting day and men with their dogs were scattered over the countryside. "What are you after?" I asked one hunter standing by the path. "Partridge and rabbit," he said.

I had a café stop in the village of Alvorge and when the man tending the bar discovered I was British he told me with pride that the two retired couples at one table were also British. I went over to say hello. They all lived locally and one of the women had been born in Gwaelod-y-Garth near Cardiff. All seemed happy and had taken a conscious decision to live away from the coast and its tourist crowds. Their presence in this part of Portugal seemed a sign of the relative vigour here of village life, compared with some dying communities I had seen further north.

After two more overnight stops, in Ansião and Caxarias, I finally drew close to Fátima. The last stretch, after night had fallen, was a long climbing hill and I was very happy to arrive. From Coimbra it had been a four-day hike of close to 120 kilometres.

I settled into a café. Was I still in rural Portugal? On one table near me a young man worked on a laptop. Most of the customers were young women. The menu offered unheard of possibilities like guava milkshake and crêpes with fruit. Normally, rural Portugal is not big on choice. In a typical restaurant, the waitress will come over and tell you that the options are beef with potatoes or salt cod with potatoes. Everywhere there are the two standard beers, Sagres and Super Bock, and of course local wine. The median age in a small town café is over 50 and there is never a laptop in sight. I was all in favour of a young, cosmopolitan Fátima. It was just utterly different from the rural Portugal to which I had grown accustomed. Suddenly I was in a different world. In my hotel the main language was Spanish and this too was a novelty.

I am not a practising Christian and I did not excel in the role of Fátima pilgrim. I need to tread respectfully here. Over the decades millions of people have gone on pilgrimages to Fátima and I am sure have drawn nourishment from the journey. I experienced overload, intellectual and emotional, and I tried to work out why.

I think the overload was partly due to the sheer physical size of the Shrine and partly to what I experienced as complex messaging. I found it impossible to use my usual technique while travelling of limiting the amount of experience I had in any one day. Fátima comes as one Big Experience Package, rather like the Manhattan skyline. But whereas the Manhattan skyline, for me, is an uplifting celebration of human energy, Fátima is a celebration of God and I personally could not relate to this way of celebrating the divine.

So, first the size of the place. It took my breath away when I first gazed on the great expanse of tarmac at the Shrine of Fátima, bigger than anything you would normally see outside of an international airport. There are basilicas at both ends of this tarmac. The more recent of the two is the round modernist Basilica da Santissima Trinidade. I sat alone in this basilica, built to accommodate 8,633 people. Does God really want places of worship as big as this? The other basilica, de Nossa Senhora do Rosário, is more modest in scale, a gracious white building with the tombs of the three children who saw the apparitions of the Virgin Mary at Fátima back in 1917.

I could see that in logic the scale of pilgrimage meant the site had to have big facilities. According to the information service of the Shrine of Fátima, about 10 million pilgrims arrived in 2017, the 100th anniversary of the apparitions, and in a normal year about six million come. I am talking here about my personal reaction to the scale of things.

Then there is the messaging, which raised so many questions that my head started to spin. At one entrance to the Shrine there is a chunk of the Berlin Wall, with an inscription next to it quoting words uttered by Polish-born Pope John Paul II in Fátima in 1991.

"Thank you, heavenly shepherd, for having guided the peoples to freedom with motherly affection." (This is my translation of the Portuguese text: "Obrigado, celeste pastora por terdes guiado com carinho maternal os povos para a liberdade.")

I reacted with scepticism to the twinning of these two themes, the Virgin Mary and the fall of the Berlin Wall. An old friend who is a Roman Catholic has since helped me with historical context. The connection apparently lies in the second of the three "secrets" or prophecies which the three children said the Virgin Mary gave them during the apparitions. The eldest child wrote these up many years later. The second "secret" was couched in oracular language but was taken to refer to communism in Russia. The children said they were told if Russia was consecrated to the Virgin and a particular programme of prayers instituted, the evil in the end would be brought down. Pope Pius II was very influenced by this and consecrated Russia to the Virgin in 1952. During the 1950s and 1960s Sunday Mass in every Roman Catholic church in the world was concluded with prayers for the conversion of Russia. Pope John Paul II, deeply influenced by Fátima, carried out a second consecration to the Virgin in 1984.

John Paul II is psychically very present at Fátima. The bullet that nearly killed him in St Peter's Square on 13 May 1981 – anniversary of the first Fátima apparition – is now part of the statue of Our Lady of Fátima at the very heart of the shrine (the Capela das Apariçoes). The bullet has been inserted into Our Lady's crown.

Fátima for me was a challenging experience. I felt very alone. Where had Portugal gone? Suddenly the language I was hearing most was Spanish, because in my hotel there were Spanish-speaking women pilgrims playing cards, loudly, for hour after hour. Travellers need to be flexible and perhaps this centre of mass pilgrimage held up a mirror to show me the limits to my flexibility. I am not an atheist, but I cannot relate to the divine amidst the tarmacked grandeur of Fátima.

CHAPTER 10

The Pulse of Middle Portugal

From Fátima I headed east on a 30-kilometre waymarked route to the town of Tomar, which is astride the pilgrims' way from Lisbon to Santiago de Compostela in Spain. The Fátima to Tomar spur, marked with yellow signs for Santiago, is called the "caminho nascente" (rising path), because you are walking in the direction of the rising sun. The route was mainly quiet country roads with some woodland tracks.

The prosperity of Fátima soon gave way to the kind of Portuguese village I had seen so often, with stone houses falling down, deserted streets and a general air of abandonment. It wasn't all desolation; there were signs of life like a café or a well-tended garden. On one occasion I spotted a boy, aged perhaps nine or 10, helping with the olive harvest. It was the first time in Portugal that I had seen a child busy on a farm.

The glory of this route is the remarkable aqueduct of Pegões, just west of Tomar, and I didn't want to miss that. I spent a night in a pilgrims' hostel in the village of Fungalvaz so that I could walk past the aqueduct in broad daylight the next morning. The hostel, right next to the church, was well-equipped and even boasted a bottle of Scotch whisky in the kitchen.

The Pegões aqueduct was worth the wait. In late morning it came into view on my left, an extraordinary six-kilometre-long stone structure with two levels of arches snaking its way through the countryside. It was built between 1593 and 1614 to take water to Tomar's Convento de Cristo.

I walked into Tomar in bright sunshine and children were skating on a small ice rink in the town's main square. It all felt suitably festive in the run-up to Christmas. I immediately took a liking to Tomar, a pretty town with swans and ducks gliding on the river Nabão and a rich history rooted in the traditions of the medieval Knights Templar. I had occasion to mention them in my account of the invention of Portugal. They began as an order of poor monks – one early symbol of the Templars showed two men riding one horse – and evolved into an elite fighting force during the Crusades. Having accumulated wealth and power, the Knights Templar came to a horrible end in the early 14th century at the hands of a French king and in popular fiction they are sometimes portrayed as villains.

In Tomar, however, they are highly revered. A statue of Dom Gualdim Pais, the Templar Grand Master who founded the town in the 12th century, dominates Tomar's main square. The Templar cross, narrow at the centre and broad at the periphery, adorns the pavements. The town's newspaper, predictably enough, is O Templário.

In the rest of Europe the Templars were annihilated, but Portugal followed its own path. After the Templars were abolished by papal Bull in 1312, in Portugal they rose again under the protection of King Dinis I, with the new name of the Order of Christ. They were very powerful in medieval Portugal and helped to finance the voyages of the Age of Discoveries.

A papal Bull of 1456 conferred on the Order, headed at that time by Prince Henry the Navigator (1394-1460), spiritual jurisdiction of all the regions conquered by Portugal now or in future "from Capes Bojador and Nun, by way of Guinea and beyond, southwards to the Indies".

Above the town is the Convento de Cristo, the Templars' former headquarters. This is one of the extraordinary buildings of Western Europe, a very atmospheric complex of chapels and cloisters set within 12th century walls. The Charola, a 16-sided Templar church adorned with 16th century wall paintings, is the jewel in the crown. Legend has it that the circular design enabled knights to attend Mass while on horseback.

Tomar is in the heart of Portugal. After visiting the Convento de Cristo, I decided to step back from the day-to-day walking and sightseeing to listen to Portuguese opinions on the state of the nation. To get some independent views I talked to Isabel Miliciano, the director of O Templário and the newspaper's only full-time journalist. I discovered that she had some very firm judgments on Portugal, which she described as being in crisis.

"I see two serious problems in Portugal – the destruction of production, and corruption," she said. Much of our conversation in the small office of O Templário concentrated on these two themes.

She spoke of Portugal's brush with bankruptcy after the financial crisis of 2008 and said that globalisation had led to the closure of many Portuguese factories. "We here in Tomar had many paper factories. We produced paper since the 19th century. Textiles, we had a textiles factory that was one of the first in Europe, the Fiação factory which had 1,500 workers. Everything has closed. During the last 15 to 20 years they gradually closed. The last paper factory closed last year (2017). It was called Prado. Today we are importing paper from Spain and other countries.

"All of this meant that our country went into an economic recession. Our politicians and high Portuguese financiers became corrupt. We had one prime minister taken prisoner. He is still to go on trial…"

Miliciano was referring to former Socialist prime minister José Sócrates, who in November 2014 was arrested at Lisbon's airport as part of the biggest corruption investigation in Portuguese history, Operation Marquis. Three years later he was indicted on graft and money laundering charges. The indictment said he had received millions of euros from a scheme involving the disgraced former bosses of the Espírito Santo banking empire and Portugal Telecom, which have both ceased to exist. Sócrates has denied the charges. In all, 19 individuals from the country's elite were charged.

(In April 2021, more than six years after the arrest of Sócrates, Portugal's criminal court for preliminary hearings dismissed the corruption accusations against him. It ruled that he would stand trial only on lesser charges of money laundering and falsifying documents.)

In our conversation, Miliciano painted a picture of a country that had been on the brink of bankruptcy and received a reprieve, both from a big international rescue package of loans in 2011 and from the boom in tourism. But she still worried about Portugal's longer-term future.

She touched on the theme of the continuing brain drain from Western Europe's poorest country. "German companies come here to recruit engineers," she said. "The United Kingdom comes to look for nurses…Our country makes the effort to train good professionals, but afterwards it doesn't get the benefit from them. It lets them leave."

Finally we touched on the phenomenon of Portugal's falling population. Miliciano is well acquainted with Tomar's population statistics since her newspaper publishes the births and deaths in the municipality. She said that every year about 500 people died in Tomar, while between 200 and 250 were born. She said couples were often reluctant to have children because of the financial cost.

"We earn money just to eat, to pay the rent," she said. "We don't build up a reserve."

The number of people on Tomar's electoral roll, she said, had dropped by about 3,000 since 2011. Now, so in 2018, Tomar had a population of about 35,000, divided equally between the town and the surrounding countryside.

It was sobering to listen to this downbeat assessment from Miliciano. Tomar, after all, is in a very fertile region, the Ribatejo, watered by the river Tagus. I walked out from O Templário and into a museum hosting an exhibition on the wildfires that ravaged Portugal in 2017, causing at least 116 deaths and burning 520,000 hectares of forest. This represented nearly 60 percent of the forests burned in the entire European Union. In the museum I talked to Filipe Martins, who had helped to take some of the photos for the exhibition. He too was downbeat, echoing themes developed by Miliciano. "We are not producing anything. We are leaving our land abandoned," said the 28-year-old, a student of photography. On a scale of zero to 10, how did he gauge the economic and social wellbeing of Portugal? He gave the country a three. Would he stay in Portugal when he graduated? "I would like to stay in Portugal, but if I got a better opportunity than here I would probably go," he said.

Seeing a welcoming Union Jack on the door of an estate agent's office, I dropped in and talked to Patricia Henriques. It is an estate agent's vocation to be upbeat and she was. From her perspective business was good, but she did note that foreigners accounted for about one third of her clients. She had British, Brazilian, Australian and French buyers in particular. Without them, things would be quiet. "I joke that Portugal is being sold off to foreigners," she said, hastening to add that this was better than houses falling down. She was more optimistic than the student about the state of the country, giving it six out of 10.

My own interim judgment, having walked through about half of the country, is that Portugal has one great strength and one great weakness. Its strength is a certain laid-back, super-relaxed quality, an ability not to get too bothered about problems. Its great weakness is that selfsame laid-back philosophy. This produces real difficulties, highlighted by the newspaper director Miliciano, including a glacial judicial system and an economy shrinking dramatically in diversity. The slow death of so many inland villages can be viewed as a sign of drift, of a country that is sleepwalking into the unknown. There are some voices in Portugal sounding an alarm. Parliamentary deputy Luis Leite Ramos has warned that two-thirds of the country could become depopulated. In fairness, Portuguese governments have set up policies to attract immigrants, offering tax concessions to incomers. Still, in my view Portugal is a continuing experiment in trying to strike the right balance, seeking to make its preference for a laid-back approach not a vice but a virtue.

When I left Tomar centre and walked south out of the town I saw with my own eyes what Miliciano had stressed – the closure of industry. One big building after another was abandoned. At a former cement works a little south of Tomar there was a still a table and two chairs in the reception office at the entrance. Economic decline is part of the ebb and flow of human affairs, but there is always something arresting about stillness where once there was bustle.

To walk long distances and then write about the experience is, perforce, to be a generalist. My journey on foot from Tomar to the sea, about 170 kilometres, evoked so many different themes that the main overarching thread was variety. I walked through the alluvial plain of the Tagus, but the river itself was only intermittently in sight and did not often serve as companion.

I was in the region called the Ribatejo, the only province of Portugal that has neither a coastline nor a border with Spain. It felt distinctive, set in its ways, moving to established rhythms. The

Ribatejo is the heartland of Portuguese bullfighting and sinuous statues of bulls and bullfighters were a staple in the towns. Cafés and restaurants sometimes featured posters, photographs or paintings inspired by the rich lore of the bullring.

My favourite was a painting of a bullfighter, on the wall of a small café. He was seated, arms akimbo and his hands resting on his thighs. He had dark hair and a brooding macho gaze. He was so totally at odds with the spirit of the age, as expressed in northern Europe at least, that perversely I rather warmed to him. Portuguese bullfighters do not kill bulls, in their variant of the tradition.

It took me three days to walk from Tomar to the old riverside city of Santarém, which I had earmarked as a place to break my journey to Lisbon with a full day's rest. I walked via Entroncamento, a nondescript town, and it was only on the second day that I felt a magic in the land.

Walking south on the Lisbon to Santiago de Compostela pilgrim way, I came upon an exquisite tree-lined avenue. Avenues of trees are where humankind meets nature in creative embrace; they are an expression of human commitment to a particular patch of earth. At least that is what my romantic soul likes to think. As I walked along the avenue, I got closer to a large mansion house and finally I realised that the mansion was shuttered and deserted. It still seemed to be intact, but a man I met told me that the house had been empty for decades. On the outside wall was a blue tile panel depicting a group of men – it looked to my untutored eye as if the tiles could be several hundred years old.

Beyond the house was a complex of outbuildings and they were falling down. Further on again was a village where, once upon a time, estate workers had lived. Now there were few residents left.

For me the Quinta da Cardiga estate, a site once owned by the Knights Templar, perfectly summed up the Portuguese countryside – beauty and decay side by side. Historically, the Portuguese poured prodigious energy into building an empire, in Africa, Asia and the Americas. This empire no longer exists. So will the Portuguese now be putting more of their energy into preserving historical gems like this in their own backyard?

I walked on, through the town of Golegã, which called itself "the capital of the horse". There were some very fine equine specimens in the fields I passed, but Golegã like other inland towns in Portugal seemed not to be faring so well with people. In the high street I spotted an undertaker's and a pharmacy, core needs of an ageing population, but not much commerce beyond that.

By evening I reached Azinhaga, an altogether different town with an air of wellbeing. I checked into a small private hostel catering to pilgrims. In this cosy establishment with a roaring log fire I met a couple from Bavaria, walking with a tent in the depths of winter to Santiago de Compostela. They were not practising Christians, but they told me that they had undertaken the pilgrimage as a gesture of support for a female friend who was sick.

Going through Azinhaga the next morning, by a fluke I walked right past the house where the author José Saramago was born. Saramago (1922-2010) is the only Portuguese-language author to have won the Nobel Prize for Literature. Portugal has had a complex relationship with the man, who was himself far from straightforward. More than 20,000 people attended his funeral in Lisbon and for some Portuguese he is a national treasure. But Saramago fell out with a number of people in this Catholic country when he published his novel *The Gospel According to Jesus Christ* which portrayed God as malicious. When the Portuguese government, reflecting Catholic opinion, blocked the book's nomination for a literary prize, Saramago left his native land and spent his final years on the Spanish island of Lanzarote.

Saramago, who lived for much of his life under a right-wing Portuguese dictatorship, was a committed communist. He was also a powerful, prolific novelist and a self-described pessimist. His novels are not easy. Often the reader is confronted with pages of unbroken text because Saramago didn't use paragraphs. He didn't use quotation marks either.

One of his best-known novels is *Blindness,* a harrowing story that describes an outbreak of contagious blindness in an unnamed country and the pitiless government response to the plague. He won his Nobel Prize for his parables "sustained by imagination, compassion and irony" and his scepticism about official truths. One of his later novels, *The Cave,* combines a savage critique of the consumer society with a tender celebration of love blossoming between a widower in his sixties and a recently widowed neighbour. When Saramago himself was in his sixties, he met and married the Spanish journalist Pilar del Río, a huge influence on the last two decades of his life. Pilar gave him loving companionship and translated many of his works into Spanish.

Saramago also wrote a travel book, *Journey to Portugal.* In it he always referred to himself as "the traveller". He was a traveller with attitude. Of one picturesque town he wrote: "The traveller would have liked Óbidos to be rather less floral." I read this complaint about an excess of flowers and decided that authors had the right to a dose of impishness. A few pages later came a broadside against the English, prompted by some tourists from England declining to eat the local fish. "A large group of English tourists has just come into the Gaivota restaurant. Nearly all of them ask for steak. The Saxons are still barbarians."

After this outburst, my readiness to indulge the writer wilted and I put Saramago down as a grumpy middle-aged man. (He wrote *Journey to Portugal* before he met Pilar, the love of his life.) Reading him prompted me to formulate a commandment for travel writers: Thou shalt not get too grumpy, too often. I am not alone in having reservations about this particular work. Author Michael

Pye, reviewing the English-language edition of *Journey to Portugal* for the New York Times, wrote: "You can carry it to Portugal, but only as a guide to Saramago himself."

I walked on through the rich flat lands of the Tagus plain and by early evening reached Santarém, an old city perched on a hill on the west bank of the river. I entered the lower part of the city, Ribeira de Santarém, and found myself walking in a slum area, through streets where the houses were either without roofs and empty, or inhabited but in a parlous state of repair. I later saw one of the roofless properties offered for sale in an estate agent's window. True to the buoyant temperament of their breed, the estate agents had found a selling point for this wreck. "Free parking," declared the advert triumphantly.

In the upper part of the town the building stock was in better shape, but still not great. The sweetly named Damascene Rose Theatre was a melancholy sight, with all its windows missing. Santarém's chief attraction is the Portas do Sol (Gates of the Sun), a garden on an old Moorish citadel commanding views of the river below. The city fathers had apparently made an effort a few years earlier but then the initiative faded. There were now light installations abandoned on the ground.

While I was in the city, the local Correio de Ribatejo newspaper ran this front-page headline – "Tourism is Santarém's strategic bet." Tourism? Now there's an idea. Santarém is a reminder that cities do not spontaneously re-invent themselves. There has to be dreaming, visioning, planning and doing. Perhaps in Santarém a new dream has begun. When I walked south out of the city on my continuing journey to Lisbon I went through a new residential area with high-rise blocks. This was by far the tidiest part of Santarém, a city with a split personality.

It took me four days to reach the outskirts of Lisbon from Santarém. I went at a leisurely pace, through a varying landscape

that was largely given over to farming. I walked with the smell of cabbage in my nostrils one moment and then looking out over long rows of vines the next. What I enjoyed most in this landscape was the sight of two colonies of storks, one in a group of trees and the other in a big country house. Storks didn't use to stay in Portugal for the winter – until about 20 years or so ago they migrated to Africa. But now, it seems, the food waste put out by humans has provided the storks with year-round sustenance. Changing the migration patterns of birds is not something that humans should be doing, but it was cheering to see them. Storks are beautiful creatures, ancient symbols of birth, rebirth and fertility.

Before I describe my brief time in Lisbon, I feel the need to digress. Inspired by Saramago's testy comments about the Saxons, I'd like to dig deeper into the subject of Portugal's ties with England.

CHAPTER 11

The World's Oldest Allies

At street level, it's the red pillar-boxes that give the game away, that and the widespread use of English. On my walk from Tomar to Lisbon I passed a public library, in the town of Vila Franca de Xira. It caught my eye because close to the entrance was a photo of Albert Einstein with a large caption in English. "The only thing that you absolutely have to know is the location of the library." This stood out in big letters, while alongside in small print were Einstein's words translated into Portuguese.

England and Portugal are often dubbed the world's oldest allies and a palpable sense of the historic links between them hangs in the air. As a Briton, I never feel completely abroad in Portugal. The Portuguese and the British are different in character, but their stories have been so intertwined that Portuguese history without the British is unimaginable.

There is nothing in European history quite like the alliance between Portugal and England. Both countries, on the physical edges of Western Europe, took to the seas and became for a while, at different times, the richest nations on earth. Their alliance encompassed the period which included first the rise and fall of the Portuguese Empire and then the rise and fall of the British Empire. There seems to be some kinship at work.

Let's look at the dynamics and the history of this alliance, which has had very rocky patches. From the Portuguese perspective, it must have felt at times like an uncomfortably tight embrace. The British, from their vantage point of greater strength, tend to look at the relationship through rose-tinted spectacles. They generally have no idea of the pain the Portuguese have suffered at times on account of policies formulated or endorsed by London. British voices have accentuated the positive. Independent Portugal and Britain have never been at war and Winston Churchill paid tribute to an alliance "without parallel in world history".

Underlying the political friendship have been considerations of realpolitik. England and Portugal were first pushed into one another's arms by their conflicts with Castile. For Portugal, England became a protector shielding it from the unwanted advances of Spain. For England, Portugal was a heaven-sent friend on the European continent as it jousted over the centuries with Spain and France.

In 1385, England stepped into the role of ally, sending archers to Portugal to counter a threat from neighbouring Castile. At the Battle of Aljubarrota, celebrated by Portugal as a key military victory guaranteeing its independence, English longbowmen fought on the right wing of the Portuguese forces. The following year, 1386, came the seminal treaty that anchored this alliance. It was ratified at Windsor when Richard II ruled England and King John I reigned in Portugal. All the way back then, the treaty embraced freedom of movement – the subjects of either monarch had the right to live in the territory of the other.

The Treaty of Windsor was sealed by a royal marriage in Porto in 1387 between King John I and Philippa of Lancaster, daughter of John of Gaunt. One of their eight children was Prince Henry the Navigator, who became an exemplar of Portuguese nationalism. (Interestingly, this marriage and its offspring is the sole reference made to England in the history section on the website of the Portuguese Embassy in London.)

In medieval times there were strong trade links between Portugal and the British Isles. What Portugal had to offer, produce like wine, olive oil, raisins and cork, was best sold into north European markets. Evidence of the ties comes partly from archaeology. Across South Wales, for example on the Newport Medieval Ship, there have been finds of 15th century copper-alloy Portuguese coins.

The one period when England and Portugal were enemies was from 1580 to 1640, when Portugal was forced into a dynastic union with Spain. One episode from this period of hostility was the English theft of an entire Portuguese library. In 1596, after taking part in the Anglo-Dutch sack of Cadiz, the Earl of Essex dropped into Faro in the Algarve for a spot more pillaging. He stole a collection of books from the city's bishop and gave it to his friend Thomas Bodley. The manuscripts, which included Portugal's first printed book, a Hebrew Old Testament, became part of the Bodleian Library at Oxford University. The theft is remembered today on a plaque in the heart of Faro. Apparently the Portuguese government has never asked to have the books back. One man who served with Essex on this expedition was the metaphysical poet John Donne. Did he lend a hand in the whole sorry affair in Faro?

Over the centuries the alliance endured, sometimes overriding sharp ideological differences. In 1654 the Protestant republic of Oliver Cromwell negotiated a treaty with Catholic Portugal which gave the Englishmen living there a number of privileges, including immunity from investigation by the Inquisition. The treaty also gave English merchants financial privileges, such as tax exemptions. Historian C.R. Boxer quotes the Marquis d'Abrantes describing the accord decades later as "the most pernicious that ever had been made with a crowned head".

After the Restoration, Charles II took a Portuguese wife, Catherine of Braganza, who famously took tea to England and made it fashionable in her adopted land. The marriage did its bit to chip away at Portugal's dominions, because the dowry included Bombay and Tangier.

Economic ties between the two drew closer. In the 17th century English workers and looms were brought in to boost Portugal's domestic woollens industry. With the Brazilian gold rush that gathered pace in the 18th century, Portugal began to import more of the precious metal than any European country had ever extracted from a territorial possession. Much of this gold went from Lisbon to England in the Falmouth Packet. In law, the export of gold from Portugal was strictly forbidden. But the Falmouth Packet, a creation of the British post office, was officially exempt from search. British warships too had a habit of dropping into Lisbon and picking up some contraband gold before they headed home.

In some counties of England, Portugal and Brazil gold coins were in wider circulation than English sovereigns. Boxer quotes an Exeter man as saying in 1713: "We have hardly any money current among us but Portugal gold." Historians estimate that about two-thirds of Brazilian gold production in the 18th century ended up in England.

The gold propelled a dramatic growth in English exports of woollen goods to Portugal and England's overall trade with Portugal was, by some estimates, greater than that of all its rivals combined. The English merchants in Lisbon grew fat and were much resented by the Portuguese.

In the 18th century, a group of Portuguese exposed to foreign ideas chafed at Portugal's failure to modernise and grew restless under what they saw as English tutelage. They were dubbed the *estrangeirados* (the foreignised ones). One leading *estrangeirado*, the diplomat Dom Luís da Cunha, called Portugal "the best and most profitable colony of England".

In the early 19th century, at least for a while, Portugal really did become a de facto British colony. Napoleon's forces invaded Portugal and the Peninsular War brought Britain into a central role in the country's affairs. For the Portuguese monarchy, the great drama of the Napoleonic period was the decision to flee to its colony of Brazil. During three hectic days in November 1807, a stream of carriages brought passengers and baggage to the quaysides of Lisbon. More than 10,000 people climbed aboard ships with hours to spare. The ships sailed on November 29 and French troops led by General Junot arrived at Lisbon the very next morning.

The thinking behind the royal exodus was to deny legitimacy to the Napoleonic invaders. Britain undertook to ensure the flight of the Portuguese court in exchange for more commercial concessions. British warships escorted the elite of Portugal, travelling with imperial regalia, government paperwork and the royal carriage, on uncomfortable lice-ridden ships to Brazil. British forces helped to drive Junot out of Lisbon.

The following year, in August 1808, Sir Arthur Wellesley, the future Duke of Wellington, landed in Portugal and defeated Junot's forces. Britain and France signed the Convention of Sintra, allowing the Napoleonic forces to return home. The convention also allowed the French to take their loot with them and this caused uproar in Portugal and England. The Portuguese are still cross about their loss of cultural heritage, as hostel-keeper Fausto Araújo reminded me in Guimarães.

But British knowhow protected Lisbon from Bonaparte's troops and even began, on Portuguese soil, the whole process of turning the tide of war against Napoleon. When the French invaded again, Wellington ordered the building of an extraordinary defence system. In secret, over the space of nearly a year, the British built three lines of defences north of Lisbon known as the Lines of Torres Vedras. North of these lines Wellington ordered a scorched earth policy. With starvation and disease thinning their ranks, the French eventually beat a retreat.

Meanwhile, in Lisbon, Britain occupied the political void left by the departure of the Portuguese royal family. What unfolded was a familiar story of the popular liberator morphing into the hated occupier. General William Beresford, picked by Britain to train the Portuguese army, sailed to Brazil in 1815 to obtain broader powers from the Portuguese prince regent. Beresford behaved like a colonial viceroy and anti-British feelings grew. Eventually, after he made a second visit to Brazil to try to shore up his political position, the mood in Lisbon swung decisively against him. Hatred of Britain spawned the Liberal Revolution of 1820 and Beresford was not allowed back into Lisbon.

When Saramago spluttered about "Saxon barbarians", he was not the first Portuguese writer to vent his spleen against the English. Eça de Queirós, the pre-eminent novelist of 19th century Portugal, dealt with the English in his book *Letters from England*. Eça spent 15 years in Victorian England as a diplomat and so had plenty of opportunity to study the people. In his book, he seems both fascinated and repelled by them. He certainly conveys with relish England's vitality, at one point giving a list of 32 travel books with titles like *Through Asia Minor on Horseback* and *The Lands of the Matabele,* which all appeared in the space of days.

But he also pours contempt on the English. "A strange people," he writes, "for whom it is out of the question that anyone can be moral without reading the Bible, be strong without playing cricket or be a gentleman without being English.

"This is what makes them detested. They never merge, they never shed their Englishness."

In Eça's day, Britain was the world's super-power, while Portugal's glory days were well past. Predictably, when it came to the European scramble for Africa, the interests of Britain and

Portugal collided. In the rows over territory, Portugal had some history on its side. After all, the Portuguese had discovered the mouth of the Congo River back in 1482, when the English were fighting the Wars of the Roses with nary a thought for Africa. Portugal aspired to a swathe of territory linking its colony of Angola in the west to Mozambique in the east. This aspiration, known as the Pink-Coloured Map, meant pushing a claim to most of what is now Zimbabwe and Zambia.

But events did not go Portugal's way. The discovery of gold in the Transvaal's Witwatersrand brought one determined player into the game, the British mining magnate Cecil Rhodes. He was alert to possible new gold rushes further north in Africa, in the areas claimed by the Portuguese. Playing on anti-Catholic sentiment in Britain, Rhodes began a propaganda campaign against Portugal.

"Rhodes' aims were an unscrupulous desire for gold, which proved to be a bubble," wrote the late Prof H. V. Livermore, a specialist in Iberian history.

On 11 January 1890 Britain informed Portugal that it wanted Portuguese troops stationed in the contested areas of Central Africa to leave. This request, clearly backed by an unspoken threat of force, is known as the British Ultimatum and it sent shockwaves through Lisbon. Portugal's government, humiliated by its own ally, had no choice. After the climbdown, anti-British fervour swept through Lisbon. One cartoonist caught the mood with a depiction of John Bull standing on African soil and firing a blunderbuss at two male figures representing Portugal. Sentiment also flared against the Portuguese monarchy and the republican press trumpeted "Treason".

Rhodes could never have foreseen the ramifications of his lobbying to curb Portuguese ambitions in Africa. The humiliation of the country and its ruling monarchy contributed to the erosion of royal authority. This reached a climax in 1908 with the assassination of both Portugal's King and Crown Prince. The country became a republic two years later.

Portugal's national anthem, *A Portuguesa*, comes from this moment of anti-British feeling in 1890 and it originally contained the line "Against the Britons, march on, march on". In 1957 these words were replaced with "Against the cannons, march on, march on".

In the 20th century, one story needs to be told and that is Portugal's contribution to Allied victory in the Second World War. While Salazar kept Portugal out of the fighting, he definitely strengthened the Allied cause. He is credited with helping to keep Spain neutral, which in itself was a big factor. Also, after years of resistance to Allied demands, Salazar finally agreed to two key Allied requests – use of airbases in the Azores and a halt to tungsten exports to Nazi Germany. Tungsten was used by the Nazis in munitions, therefore Portugal's export of this rare metal to Germany in exchange for gold was, while it lasted, a very sore point in London. The all-important ability to use airfields in the Azores helped the Allies to win the war in the Atlantic.

There is one murky aspect to this decision by Salazar to grant these two requests. Martin Page, in *The First Global Village, How Portugal Changed the World,* refers to one question mark hanging over the Portuguese turnaround. Page writes that at the same time as Salazar's concessions to the Allies, his police, apparently acting on accurate tip-offs, rounded up some anti-Salazar activists. British agents, he writes, have since denied that these arrests were part of any trade-off. One intriguing element is that writer Graham Greene was at this point a spy working for Britain's Secret Intelligence Service (MI6) and he ran British spy operations in Portugal. Greene resigned from his MI6 post after the Portuguese arrests and went on to write *Our Man in Havana,* a black comedy of death and betrayal that drew on the Portugal phase of his spying career. It paints an unflattering picture of Britain's secret service.

So it's an alliance that has followed a long and winding road. But the story has overall been positive and the fruits of the Treaty of Windsor can still be seen, with about 40,000 Britons officially residing in Portugal and approximately 250,000 Portuguese living in Britain. Even as Britain prepared to leave the European Union, the country remained the most popular destination for Portuguese emigrants.

CHAPTER 12

Lisbon, City of Light

In the space of just a few years, Lisbon has become a hot ticket. It has turned into a top destination, a world city. So what is the secret of its charm? Lisbon is gloriously walkable, a cityscape just to wander in without ticking off a list of tourist attractions. Lisbon's position at the mouth of the Tagus and its extensive waterfront, give both a sense of spaciousness and a connection to momentous events in history. This was Europe's point of departure to the wider world. It was from these shores that the first Europeans sailed around the southern tip of Africa to India.

The way I experience Lisbon, this sense of spaciousness is linked not only to the water but also to big changing skies and wonderful light. Portugal can do vivid deep-blue skies with not a cloud in sight. But Lisbon insists on variety – it does sunshine sometimes, but it also does cloud and rain.

I first came to Lisbon in the mid-1980s. When I try to connect the fragments of memory I have from that visit I fail to match them up with the city I experienced in 2018 and 2019. The Lisbon of the 1980s had no buzz; it felt rather subdued, outshone by other European capitals.

Now the world is beating a path to its door. Colourful street art engages the eye and enhances the sense of a city determined not to be dull. In 2018, about 70,000 people came to the Portuguese capital for the international tech gathering called the Web Summit. In summer the city overflows with tourists – book ahead if you want to have a bed. Even in winter visitors are a common sight. On Boxing Day 2018, three cruise liners were moored in Lisbon harbour.

Lisbon has become so cosmopolitan that it springs surprises. I walked into the centre of Lisbon from the northern residential suburbs and threaded my way through the labyrinth of Alfama, the hilly Lisbon district of narrow alleys and bijou restaurants. Outside one restaurant stood a young woman seeking to entice passers-by into the eatery. She engaged me in conversation, speaking English. I replied in Portuguese and she told me that she didn't speak Portuguese; she was from Nepal. So my first conversation in central Lisbon was with a person, working in tourism, who knew no Portuguese. Her employers presumably felt that English was the only language that mattered.

One very different memory I have from Alfama is coming across two children kicking a ball around in the street. In how many European capitals do you see that? So, cosmopolitan it may be, but Lisbon is still a city where local people can bring up families in time-honoured ways and use backstreets as a playing field.

I arrived in central Lisbon on December 20. After walking about 870 kilometres, I was just in time to make a crucial purchase for a family Christmas. My daughters Jô, Megan and Rachel were due to fly in from London and the main task allotted to me was to buy the turkey. The Portuguese, with their boundless dedication to salt cod, tend to have that as their Christmas dish, but we were going to follow British tradition. I sought advice from a restaurant on where to buy a turkey and they directed me to a well-stocked food shop in central Lisbon that was happy for me to order a bird. I breathed a sigh of relief. Soon after, my daughters arrived and we all took up residence in a comfortable high-ceilinged apartment with views over the shimmering waters of the Tagus.

There is, of course, a big shift from a solo walk to a family holiday, a move to collective decision-making. One easy decision was to undertake a family pilgrimage to the Museu Nacional do Azulejo, the National Tile Museum. This is one of Lisbon's undoubted gems, housed in a beautiful 16th century convent. Megan came across Islamic ceramics during her university studies and became a tile aficionado. One of the museum's prize exhibits is a 36m-long panel, painted blue on white, giving a great panoramic view of Lisbon before the earthquake of 1755. Megan was in tile heaven and particularly liked some blue, white and yellow geometric patterns that put her in mind of Istanbul's Topkapi Palace.

Spending time with my daughters, I set aside my walking rule. After Christmas, Megan, Rachel and I took a day trip from Lisbon to one of Portugal's busiest tourist traps, the Palácio da Pena above the town of Sintra. Rachel had enjoyed some generous draughts of Lisbon nightlife and felt a little fragile, so we took a taxi to the palace. This 19th century extravagance of onion domes and crenellated towers in bright colours features on the front cover of the *Lonely Planet* guide to Portugal. This kind of world fame carries a price; the queues were monumental. When we eventually had our tickets, inside the palace the queues continued and we all shuffled in a line from one room to the next.

But don't let me put you off Sintra. It is worth it and you're not obliged to go into the Palácio da Pena. After the palace we took in a nearby 10th century Moorish castle, with ramparts running along ridges and big wonderful views over forests and hills. From there we followed a walking trail down into Sintra, a town set in landscapes of lush greenery that has attracted writers over generations. One early visitor was Henry Fielding, the 18th century English novelist. He hired mules to get to Sintra where he rented a mansion. In a letter, he told his brother that Sintra was the best place in the world to write a novel. We walked past one house with a plaque saying that Hans Christian Andersen, the master craftsman of fairy tales, had lived there. Other writers who have spent time in Sintra include Robert Southey, William Wordsworth, Alfred Lord Tennyson, Lord Byron and Graham Greene. Sintra is easier to reach than it was in Fielding's day and there's no longer any need to hire mules. We went back to Lisbon by train.

If you are at all historically minded, part of Lisbon's appeal is its rich history. I am indebted to Barry Hatton's book *Queen of the Sea, a History of Lisbon* for many of the following tidbits.

As early as Roman times, Lisbon was a very significant city. For four centuries it was under Moorish rule but in 1147 Portugal's first king, Afonso Henriques, enlisted the help of some unruly knights who had signed up for the Second Crusade. The Crusaders, largely a mix of English, Scottish, French, Flemish and German soldiers, took the city after a 17-week siege. The fullest account of the campaign is a letter written to a man in Suffolk, probably by an Anglo-Norman priest. The letter, in Latin, gives a graphic account of medieval siege warfare, with battering rams, catapults and burning pitch.

At the end of the 15th and the beginning of the 16th century, the Age of Discoveries started to bring great change to Lisbon. When Vasco da Gama returned in 1499, after two years at sea, from his historic first voyage to India, he and King Manuel rode on horseback to cheering crowds up to St George's castle on the hill. This castle was the nerve centre of the Portuguese monarchy. But now that Portugal's fortunes were so closely linked to its maritime voyages, Manuel laid plans to build a new palace near the waterfront. This palace, the Paço da Ribeira, was just part of a complex which included a royal armoury and royal shipyards. On the ground floor of the palace was the India House, which administered trade throughout the empire and stored the spoils of this trade, from nutmeg to copper. King Manuel went to visit every day.

Lisbon grew rich on international trade, while hunger stalked the countryside. Hatton says the whole phenomenon of a mighty Lisbon playing a disproportionately large role in the life of Portugal dates from the 16th century. This was also the period when Lisbon first drew in a lot of slave labour. No other city in Europe has benefitted quite as much as Lisbon from the toil of African slaves. By the mid-16th century, Lisbon had nearly 10,000 slaves, about 10 percent of the population. On the European continent at that time, Lisbon stood alone in having such a sizeable number of Africans, almost all of them there under duress.

Lisbon is generally well endowed with museums, but as I wrote in my chapter on the Portuguese Empire, there is one yawning gap. There is nothing focused on Portugal's big role in the history of slavery. After long years of debate and delay, Lisbon did seem poised to get its first memorial to victims of slavery in the third decade of the 21st century. Lisbon council agreed to fund a memorial designed by Angolan artist Kiluanji Kia Henda. The memorial, due to stand in central Lisbon, will consist of 540 black lacquered aluminium stands representing sugar cane.

Henda has said of his design: "There is pain and tragedy in it, but there is also an open door to a better future."

In Lisbon's history, one transcendental event was the earthquake of 1755, one of the strongest to hit Western Europe in recorded history. On a holy day, All Saints' Day on November 1, three jolts brought two-thirds of Lisbon's buildings crashing down and a six-metre high tsunami rushed up the Tagus. The quake, with an epicentre under the sea south-west of Cape St Vincent, struck when Lisbon's populace was halfway through celebrating Mass in the city's 56 churches. All the lighted candles in these crowded churches helped set off raging firestorms, with temperatures reaching 1000C. These fires burned for days. Many thousands died, incinerated, crushed under the buildings, or drowned. The tsunami was so powerful that it reached the Caribbean. One of the buildings that came down was the new Royal Opera House, pet project of the reigning monarch, José I. This sumptuous six-storey building, with a gold and white interior, had been inaugurated in March.

Estimates of the number of dead vary considerably. Economic historian Alvaro Pereira has calculated that in Lisbon between 30,000 and 40,000 people perished, out of a city population of about 200,000. According to Pereira: "All in all, the 1755 earthquake and the resulting tsunami and fires caused between 40,000 and 50,000 deaths in Portugal, Spain and Morocco."

In Lisbon, by nightfall authorities had started to react and to try to save lives. "Some regard it as the first modern, centralised state response to catastrophe," wrote Hatton. The draconian clarity shaping this response sprang from the mind of chief minister Sebastião José de Carvalho e Melo. In history books he is known by his later title, the Marquis de Pombal, and we met him earlier as the moderniser of the port wine business in the Douro valley. He was effectively the ruler of Portugal. A man both ruthless and dynamic, he stands out as the pre-eminent administrator in his country's history. With Pombal at the helm, in excess of 350 pages of orders, edicts and decrees poured from the central government in the space of three days after the calamity.

To avoid the threat of disease from corpses, on Pombal's recommendation some bodies were taken out in ships and dumped at sea. The authorities hanged looters and commandeered food stocks, taking it to designated points for distribution. Bakers and millers were brought into Lisbon and food prices fixed at pre-earthquake levels. With effective measures brought in swiftly, Lisbon kept at bay both epidemics and starvation.

The destruction of Lisbon offered the opportunity to rebuild the city. What emerged from the rebuilding was a city with two quite distinct architectural styles. In the central part, the Baixa, Pombal introduced a grid system, with tidy streets running north and south. Alfama, to the east, maintained its character as a medieval warren. The result is that modern visitors to Lisbon get two cities, as it were, for the price of one.

If your time is short in Lisbon and one day's conventional sightseeing would suffice, I would ride the number 15 tram the few kilometres to Belém, on the western side of Lisbon. This contains the early 16th century Belém Tower, a limestone fortress on the water's edge which has come to symbolise the Age of Discoveries. Also in Belém is the exquisite Jerónimos Monastery, begun in 1502 and completed a century later. It was the grandest project in Portugal's golden age.

Two very different historical themes are present in this building's history. On the one hand, there is the role of slave trading in Europe's enrichment. The construction of the monastery was partly financed by Florentine banker and slaver Bartolomeo Marchionni. On the other hand, the monastery has a place in the history of the European Union. It was here that European leaders signed the 2007 Lisbon Treaty that provided a constitutional basis for the EU and for the first time gave member states the explicit legal right to leave. That's a lot of historical baggage for one monastery – from slavery to Brexit inside one set of walls.

If, after your visit, you're curious to read what writers have made of Lisbon I recommend two utterly different novels. One is *Pereira Maintains* by the Italian author Antonio Tabucchi about a Lisbon journalist wrestling with his conscience under the Salazar dictatorship. The other is José Saramago's *The Year of the Death of Ricardo Reis*. This complex novel is set in Lisbon in 1936 – so again Salazar's time – and it evokes a formal, fusty, dangerous age. It often names individual city streets and squares, so it helps if you already know Lisbon a little.

The Belém Tower, symbol of the Age of Discoveries

CHAPTER 13

Fernando Pessoa: The Man Who Never Was

One name inseparable from Lisbon is Fernando Pessoa, the poet and philosopher whose familiar dapper image, with hat, glasses, moustache and bowtie, adorns so much in Portugal from bankcards to tourist kitsch.

Pessoa's subjects as a poet range from the sea, so central to Portugal's whole sense of identity, to the universal theme of childhood. As the mood takes him, he can be tender and evocative or nihilistic and wilfully cynical. Not the most methodical of men, he left most of what he wrote unfinished or unpublished in a wooden trunk. Scholars have spent the best part of a century untangling what he left behind.

For centuries, the Portuguese revered Luís de Camões as their national poet. He sang of the glory of empire and his life, in the 16th century, seemed studded with tales of adventure. The Portuguese tell the story that shipwrecked off Cambodia he swam ashore holding above the water his unfinished epic *Os Lusíadas*.

Although the day of Camões' death, June 10, is still the country's national day, Portugal has transferred much of its literary affection to Pessoa, a man of very different cloth. Pessoa (1888-1935) was a sedentary city dweller, a creature of habit who in his adult years seldom strayed far from the café life of Lisbon. He is often seen as the embodiment of the *flâneur,* the sauntering observer of urban ways. In today's Lisbon, Pessoa still feels very present. There's a life-size bronze sculpture of him seated at a table outside the Café A Brasileira, a meeting place for intellectuals back in his day, in the district of Chiado.

Pessoa (the name means "person" in Portuguese) published little during his lifetime and he was not a household name. Today his reputation rides high. The late American literary critic Harold Bloom, in his influential book *The Western Canon,* praised the work of 26 writers who for him had shaped Western literature since the age of Dante. Pessoa was the one Portuguese-language writer admitted onto Bloom's select list. (It is, of course, a subjective list. Dostoevsky is absent and so are Pushkin, Victor Hugo, Balzac, Baudelaire and Zola.)

During his lifetime Pessoa completed only one book in Portuguese, the poem *Mensagem* (Message) published in 1934, the year before his death. But he was very active as writer, literary critic and analyst of current affairs, contributing to many Portuguese newspapers. After his death, collaborators pieced together scraps of writing he had left and published *The Book of Disquiet,* ruminations, often melancholic, on life.

Pessoa had a distinctive, turbulent childhood. When he was five his father died of tuberculosis and his mother later married a military officer who was appointed to be Portuguese Consul in Durban. In 1896, Pessoa sailed with his mother to South Africa. In a letter he once wrote that his English education there was "a factor of supreme importance in my life, and, whatever my fate be, indubitably shaping it."

The young Pessoa was bookish, brilliant and averse to all sport. His favourite reading was Shakespeare and Milton but he also devoured Dickens and European classics ancient and modern. With his family still in South Africa, Pessoa returned to Lisbon in 1905 to study diplomacy. However, dogged by illness he did not complete these studies. As a cultured young man with a sharp mind, he received offers of well-paid employment but turned them down to live his calling as a poet. He made ends meet as a commercial writer and translator.

In Lisbon, he contributed to the European intellectual currents of his day as one of the writers who created the literary magazine Orpheu. This published only two issues, in 1915, but it made its mark by introducing modernist poetry to Portugal.

When Bloom included Pessoa in his select band of Western writers, he seems to have been influenced by Pessoa's remarkable use of heteronyms. These were pen names but sometimes much, much more than traditional pseudonyms. In their fullest expression heteronyms were identities with an independent intellectual life. Brazil's José Paulo Cavalcanti Filho devotes more than a quarter of his book *Fernando Pessoa uma quase-autobiografia* to the subject of heteronyms and he lists 127, all men, invented by the poet.

Pessoa created three fully fledged heteronyms, with distinct writing styles and individual life histories. These fictional authors were Alberto Caeiro, Ricardo Reis and Álvaro de Campos. He provided each with a time and place of birth and an astrological chart. Pessoa was born under a Water sign. Caeiro, he decided, was a Fire sign, Reis Air and Campos Earth. Between them they embraced the principles of ancient wisdom; they had opinions and sometimes commented on the work of their colleagues. Reis described Caeiro as the greatest poet of the 20th century.

Caeiro was the designated Master of the heteronyms. Orphaned young, he lived most of his life in the country with a great aunt. Pessoa had him die at 26, the age of Pessoa's best friend, Mário de Sá-Carneiro, when he committed suicide. Reis was a Jesuit-educated doctor. A royalist, he emigrated to Brazil after the failure of a monarchist rebellion against the Portuguese Republic. As a writer, he focused on odes. Campos studied naval engineering in Glasgow. He was a vain man who took three hours to dress and like other writers of his time used opium and cocaine.

These three heteronyms have been absorbed into the bloodstream of Portuguese intellectual life. On Pessoa's marble tomb in Lisbon's Jerónimos monastery are engraved verses attributed to Reis, Caeiro and Campos. Not one line on the tomb is directly attributed to Pessoa. As we saw in the last chapter, Saramago wrote a novel entitled *The Year of the Death of Ricardo Reis*. In this book Saramago brought Reis back from Brazil to Lisbon, where he conversed with the ghost of Pessoa.

The description of Pessoa as "the man who never was" came originally from Portuguese-born poet and essayist Jorge de Sena. It expressed the idea that Pessoa's heteronyms crowded so eagerly onto the stage that the man himself was somehow left clinging to the shadow of a life.

In her book on the poet, his niece Manuela Nogueira gave another slant to the words "the man who never was". In *O Meu Tio Fernando Pessoa* (My Uncle Fernando Pessoa) she described a beloved uncle who could be so totally on the wavelength of children that he often seemed to be a child himself. She wrote about his habit of doing imitations of an ibis, which in ancient Egypt was associated with Thoth, god of writing, wisdom and magic. Thoth was depicted as having the body of a man and the head of an ibis. For his ibis imitations, Pessoa would stand on one leg, stick out his neck and stretch out his arms in the form of wings. The one love of Pessoa's life called him by the nickname Ibis.

Since Thoth was the god of magic, the ibis clearly had resonance for Pessoa, who had a keen interest in the occult and felt that he had powers of mediumship. Astrology in particular was a favourite pursuit. Visitors to Lisbon's Fernando Pessoa House, the building where he lived for the last 15 years of his life, literally step over Pessoa's astrological chart as they enter the museum. It is engraved into the floor. Pessoa himself, astrologically speaking, was a native of Gemini.

He had friends, but there was much of the loner in his make-up. He practically chain-smoked and drank prodigious quantities of wine and brandy, though according to his family he never appeared drunk. He was elegant and went to Lisbon's most expensive tailor for his suits and coats.

He made only one known foray into romance, wooing a 19-year-old woman named Ophelia Queiroz, whom he met at the office. Her family apparently chose the name Ophelia because a sister of hers was reading *Hamlet* on the day of her birth. Ophelia grew up to be a cultured young woman, fluent in French. She was short and slender, with dark hair and eyes, and didn't wear make-up.

Borrowing words spoken by Hamlet to his Ophelia, Pessoa declared his love for her in the office and kissed her passionately. Ophelia hoped for marriage and began to prepare her trousseau. Pessoa ended the romance 10 months later with a note to her that opened with the words "O amor passou." Love has passed. In fact love put in one more appearance, nearly a decade later, when they had a second phase to their relationship. In her letters Ophelia poured out her love, but the poet dumped her again.

With such a rich inner life, with all those heteronyms buzzing around in his head, it's perhaps not surprising that Pessoa found relationships a challenge. More broadly, the whole question of his sanity apparently took up some of his thinking. Cavalcanti, his biographer, quotes Pessoa's sister Teca as saying that all his life he was afraid of going mad like his paternal grandmother, who had very serious mental afflictions.

On the whole, contemporary Portugal seems enchanted with Pessoa, but the praise is not universal. In a 2015 interview with the Spanish newspaper El País, the Portuguese novelist António

Lobo Antunes was scathing about his compatriot. "The book of I don't know what bores me to death," he said. "The poetry of the heteronym Álvaro de Campos is a copy of Walt Whitman; and that of Ricardo Reis, of Virgil. I wonder if a man who never fucked can be a good writer."

I also found *The Book of Disquiet* not really to my taste. I kept expecting it to take wing and give me pleasure, but it never did. The nihilism grated. Here's one sentence from the book, which is true to its flavour; "To love is merely to grow tired of being alone: it is therefore both cowardice and a betrayal of ourselves (it is vitally important that we should not love)." Pessoa attributed authorship to one of his heteronyms, Bernardo Soares, but he did say that Soares was "a mutilation" of himself.

When Pessoa was on form, he was a poet touched by genius. His years in Africa inspired one remarkably evocative poem, *Un soir à Lima*. Despite the title, this was in fact a Portuguese-language poem. It describes the young Pessoa listening to his mother play the tune *Un soir à Lima* on the piano, as the African moon shone bright. The power of the poem is almost overwhelming. You are there, with Fernando Pessoa the boy, engrossed in the experience of his beloved mother making music in Africa. *Un soir à Lima* is a poem for the ages.

His book *Mensagem*, 44 poems in all, contains lyrical writing on the great figures in Portugal's age of empire and on the sea. The literary critic Bloom expressed surprise that there was no reference in *Mensagem* to the poet Camões, but Cavalcanti the biographer argues that this was deliberate on Pessoa's part. He was seeking to be the new national poet, so why give space to the old?

Having published *Mensagem*, Pessoa did not linger long on this earth. He died in Lisbon on 30 November 1935. On the previous day, Pessoa wrote his last words, in English: "I know not what tomorrow will bring." Cavalcanti believes that Pessoa died of pancreatitis and it is not too much of a stretch to say that he smoked and drank himself to death.

Cavalcanti recounts a moving postscript to Pessoa's life and to his relationship with Ophelia. In 1985, a few journalists gathered in Lisbon to cover the 50th anniversary of the poet's death. They included Brazil's Ronald de Carvalho who sought an interview with Ophelia. She gave permission for a television crew to film her at home and Carvalho returned in the evening to honour her beauty with a red rose. Having bestowed his gift he turned to leave, but Ophelia called him back and opened her heart, telling him a story the world did not know.

She said that when Pessoa died the hospital phoned her and gave her the opportunity to see his body before his family arrived. She went and said final farewells to the man she had loved her whole adult life. A nun at the hospital gave her a book that Pessoa had with him when he died, a book of sonnets by the poet Bocage, given to Pessoa by a friend with a dedication paying tribute to his talent. This Ophelia gave to the journalist, with the words "Since no-one will believe this story, I give you this copy as proof." Carvalho promised Ophelia that he would say nothing about her clandestine visit to the hospital until after her death. She died in 1991 and years later the journalist revealed her account to Cavalcanti.

A footnote: Ophelia had the good sense not to pine forever for what might have been. Three years after Pessoa's death, she married a man from the world of theatre.

CHAPTER 14

To the Whistler Tree

On the road again. I hope you are still with me after the literary digression. With strong winds whipping up the waters of the Tagus, I left Lisbon on February 1, taking a 20-minute ferry ride across the river to the town of Barreiro. It was a wrench to leave the city after two pleasurable visits. Christmas there with my three daughters had been a heart-warming change after weeks of solitary tramping. After some Portuguese travels with my daughters, I returned to Wales and sat out most of January, resting at home. Then it was back by train from Abergavenny to Lisbon to resume my walk, in the longer days of the Portuguese spring.

I returned to the fray with the spring in my step. On reaching the southern shore of the Tagus, I set my sights on walking to one particularly venerable cork oak tree, two days away to the east. Production of cork is a Portuguese success story. Export of cork was important as far back as the 14th century and nowadays Portugal accounts for half of world production.

The first day I walked mainly through built-up areas, but even so I spotted the occasional cork oak. My goal was Palmela, a pretty town with cobbled streets and a well-preserved medieval castle perched high on a crag.

Scanning a restaurant menu for dinner, my eye settled on pork Alentejo style. While travelling through northern and central Portugal I had spurned regional dishes from the south, on the grounds that they would be best sampled on home territory. Alentejo means "beyond the Tagus", the river I had crossed in the morning, so presumably I had arrived. I checked with the waitress. "This is Alentejo, yes?" "No, this is Estremadura." Nothing like travel for sharpening one's hazy ideas of geography. Alentejo apparently started a little to the east.

For the first time it struck me how prominent rivers are in the naming of historic Portuguese provinces. Estremadura means "furthest from the (river) Douro". Alentejo I have just mentioned and Ribatejo, the region I travelled through before reaching Lisbon, means "above the Tagus". Minho, in the far north, is named after the river which delineates part of Portugal's border with Spain.

After the little geography lesson from the waitress, I decided not to be purist and to plump for the pork Alentejo style. It turned out to be very tender, sweet succulent pieces of meat served with clams in their shells and potatoes. You can easily spot it on a menu – *Carne de porco à alentejana*.

On the second day out from Lisbon the landscape was much more rural and I saw literally thousands of cork oak trees. By early evening I was walking with a field on my left given over entirely to scattered cork oaks.

After nightfall I reached the town of Águas de Moura, home to the Whistler Tree, Arvore do Assobio in Portuguese. The tree is so called because of the number of songbirds that sometimes gather in its branches. In 2018 it won the European Tree of the Year award and that brought it to my attention.

The day after my arrival in Águas de Moura I had no difficulty in finding the tree, which stands in the town itself on a kind of village green with a small playground next to it and houses at a respectful distance. Signage in Portuguese and English tells the tree's story.

This cork oak, one of the oldest and biggest in the world, has yielded prodigious quantities of cork since it was planted in 1783, the year that also saw the birth of the United States. Bark has been harvested from the tree more than 20 times since 1820. In 1991, the best harvest so far, it yielded more than 1,200 kilos of cork, which is more than most trees produce in their lifetimes. This was enough to make more than 100,000 stoppers.

The signage flags up the unusual qualities of cork oaks (Quercus suber). "The cork produced by cork oak trees is a unique raw material, which floats on water and is elastic, compressible, impermeable, odourless, and with excellent insulating qualities, natural, renewable, recyclable and environmentally friendly with a millenarian past of various uses and a promising future."

The initial harvesting of bark typically happens when the tree is 25 years old, so cork oak husbandry is a prime example of what Irish author Charles Handy has called cathedral thinking, or thinking beyond an individual human life span. After that first harvest the bark comes off again every nine years or so, between May and August. Mature trees always have a number on, so "8" means the last harvest was in 2018 and the next will be due in 2027.

At the start of the millennium, the outlook for cork did not look brilliant. The wine industry, worried about the phenomenon of cork sometimes tainting their product, started switching to plastic stoppers and screw tops. But the cork industry fought back, investing in technology to reduce the risk of cork taint, a mouldy smell that can be caused by tiny fungi in the bark. Chinese imports of cork have been soaring. The manufacturers of premium wines are showing a clear preference for cork and growing awareness of the global problem of plastic pollution should help its cause.

The wine industry is not the only market for cork. Shredded cork has been used in protective thermal coating on booster rockets, including the Space Shuttle. Baseballs have a cork centre. Cork is used in footwear, lifebuoys and interior decoration – I have stayed in one hostel where the whole reception desk was made of cork. One very traditional use of the trees is to give their acorns to pigs who then provide top-quality ham.

If you come across cork oaks be sure to go up and say hello. The trunks have a monumental hardness about them.

CHAPTER 15

Évora the Enchantress

From Águas de Moura I travelled four days to reach Évora. I walked under blue skies, past carpets of flowers in the meadows, cork oaks and sturdy lambs. Portuguese spring had definitely sprung. On the second day, walking to the town of Vendas Novas, I finally entered the province of Alentejo. This part of Portugal is known for its gentle pace of life, though also for its political radicalism. The Portuguese tell jokes about the people of Alentejo, rather as the French take a dig at the Belgians or the British traditionally cracked jokes about the Irish.

Nowadays practically every settlement of any size, it seems, has worked on its branding message to the world. Vendas Novas projected pride in two very different things – its pork rolls and its artillery guns. In Portuguese the pork rolls are called *bifanas*. Nearly every café in Vendas Novas proclaimed that it had either the original *bifana* or the best. One establishment, moving with the times, even had a vegan *bifana*. I tried one *bifana* – it would have been wrong not to – and it was excellent. I started to formulate a view that Portuguese food south of the Tagus was better than its cousin to the north. Vendas Novas has pride in its guns because an artillery regiment is stationed in the town. Guns are placed in front of the regiment buildings and one stands on a roundabout on the eastern approach to town.

On the third day I walked to Montemor-o-Novo. Its castle on a hill, visible from some 10 kilometres away, set the tone for the day, gently insinuating a long, settled history. On the fourth and final day, shortly before reaching Évora, I notched up 1,000 kilometres on the road since I began the walk in Spain. I walked into Évora after nightfall and first saw its walls when I was practically upon them. I knew the city had ancient walls, but the scale, the sheer solidity of them, came as a shock. Évora is the real deal, a medieval city.

I had a hostel right in the heart of old Évora and was able to enjoy the place to the full. If you've seen Lisbon and Porto and are trying to decide which Portuguese city to visit next, Évora is a very strong candidate. Its most famous landmark is a Roman temple, commonly but wrongly called the Temple of Diana. Its university gives youth and vibrancy while its buildings and narrow alleys give a sense of a bygone age.

Roman Évora

The university, established in 1559, is one of Évora's architectural gems. It is adorned with azulejos and even the classrooms have tiles, with themes aligned with different branches of learning. The Cathedral of Évora is the biggest medieval cathedral in Portugal. Guidebooks say the flags of Vasco da Gama's fleet were blessed here before he set sail for India in 1497.

In all of Portugal's cities I found people who could talk with deep fondness and knowledge about the city where they lived. Évora was no exception. I heard that it was a pioneer in protecting architectural integrity, with the authorities decreeing from the 1930s onwards the height of buildings and what colour houses could be painted. You can feel the love in Évora.

But historically Évora has also had a dark side, as visitors are reminded by a discreet inscription in the city's main square, the Praça do Giraldo. This inscription, installed in 2016, pays tribute to the victims of the Portuguese Inquisition, but without saying who the victims were or why the tribute has been placed on this spot. The location of the plaque is simply explained. It was here in the Praça do Giraldo that the Inquisition burned those condemned to die.

To find out about the victims, I went to Évora's splendid old public library close to the Roman temple. An assistant dug out António Borges Coelho's *Inquisiçao de* Évora (The Évora Inquisition). It is a harrowing two-volume work that runs to 775 pages, with long lists of named victims. There is also analysis. Coelho's conclusion is that Jews bore the brunt of the Portuguese Inquisition's ferocity: their crime was to practise the religion of Judaism. Coelho writes that of the 438 people executed by the Inquisition in Évora between 1533 and 1668, 433 were charged with Judaism. Roman Catholic leaders have, in recent decades, apologised for the suffering caused by the Inquisition, which had separate establishments in Portugal and Spain.

There is more to the Évora region than the old city centre. Just a few kilometres out of town is a site of ancient monuments that for some is a big part of the reason to visit. In the mid-1960s, the Portuguese discovered standing stones that are now considered the most important megalithic site in the Iberian Peninsula and one of the oldest in the world. I went to see these monuments with Angola-born guide Jones Fernandes. Standing by a group of nearly 100 stones that make up the Almendres Cromlech, Fernandes said: "This was already old when Stonehenge was built." I found that a mind-expanding statement. Archaeologists reckon the cromlech is about 7,000 years old, so about 2,000 years older than Stonehenge. Fernandes stressed that in this region the hydrographic basins of three rivers meet – the Tagus, Sado and Guadiana. This, he said, helped to support a large population by Neolithic standards.

Not every visitor has been enchanted by Évora. George Borrow, that remarkable man of Norfolk who learned Welsh and wrote *Wild Wales*, was in Évora in December 1835, distributing Bibles for the Bible Society. He hit upon the strategy of simply leaving Bibles on footpaths for passers-by to pick up. Borrow, who had previously worked in Russia, complained about the cold in the city. In a letter, he wrote about Évora: "I wrap myself up in my Russian pelisse and sit with my feet over an earthen pan of charcoal; but the charcoal makes me sick without warming me and then I say: How I wish I had never left Russia."

CHAPTER 16

"We are few and old."

After walking through a chunk of Portugal, it felt time to step back once again from stage-by-stage accounts of my journey. I had my own opinions by now on the state of the countryside, but I wanted to hear the views of a Portuguese expert. Since Évora is a university city, this seemed a good place to find a qualified person for a conversation about rural Portugal. My curiosity led me to Professor Aurora Carapinha, in the University of Évora's Department of Landscape, Environment and Planning. The professor describes herself as an academic landscape architect.

We met at her university office and I asked her how she saw the general state of Portugal's countryside. "In my opinion the countryside is today one of the great problems of Portugal's reality in the 21st century, because all the policies that have been pursued for many years, since the (1974) revolution, were determinant factors in emptying the countryside, in diminishing the countryside."

"I don't think it was intentional," she said. "But the public policies, in my opinion, brought people who lived in the countryside to emigrate to Portugal's coastal zone." She said of successive governments: "They built roads, with the idea that if they built a road they would create centres of development in the interior, but these roads led people of the interior to leave for the coast because they weren't accompanied by a package of measures to improve living conditions for these populations... There is no work or there is badly paid work and people go in search of better living conditions."

She said one other aspect of government policy that had aggravated the rural exodus was the building of dams, which had reduced the area of farmland.

"There has been a whole set of policies over the years which resulted, in a first phase, in people emigrating to the big cities and then, from the north of Portugal especially, to France, Belgium and Luxembourg..."

According to European Union statistics, Portugal has the highest emigration as a proportion of the population in the EU. More than two million Portuguese people live outside of their country.

I said that in the Natural Park of Montesinho, where I first entered Portugal, the villages had no residents under 60 and it was my impression that these villages were going to die. What was the professor's opinion? "Yes, they will die, just like in the whole interior of the country because the other problem that presents itself is the problem of demographics. Today, here in Alentejo, for every five people three are older than 65. We have 19 inhabitants to a square kilometre. Historically, this was always a highly populated region... The great challenge for Portugal today is how are we going to reverse this situation in the countryside?"

"We are a rural country, but not an agricultural one," said the professor. I said that in December I had seen an elderly Portuguese couple, the husband up a ladder, the woman on the ground, struggling to bring in the olive harvest. The woman told me that their son lived in Paris, too far away to help. Expanding on this, Professor Carapinha said: "A rural country needs to have an agricultural economy but it doesn't exist, because these people in their eighties and their seventies don't have the ability to go to markets and their children are in France, England, France above all, Belgium, Luxembourg, Brazil – abroad – and they go back in summer. In summer these villages are full of people."

Inside Portugal, she saw the demographic shift to the coast becoming more pronounced. "Lisbon, Porto are great cities. Development is just along the coast and more and more that's the way it is." The authorities, she said, were closing courts, hospitals, post offices and schools in rural areas. "So how can people go and live there?"

What should the government's priorities be to address the flight from the countryside? "The first priority for the Portuguese government is to stop talking about the interior, because we are 140 kilometres wide, 200 kilometres wide. There cannot be a dichotomy between the interior and the coast. Whoever is in Madrid is in the interior of the Iberian Peninsula. Whoever is in Évora is not in the interior. I am 120 kilometres from the capital. The problem is that we have created this idea that there exists 'an interior'… Portugal is a very narrow strip. Where is the interior? If I leave Lisbon at two o'clock in the afternoon at half past four I am at Huelva (Spain) on the border. Interior? There is no interior… The politicians should think of the country as one whole."

In terms of specific policies, Professor Carapinha argued that it was extremely important to have more decentralisation of services, but without regional assemblies because the country was too small. "Portugal is the same size as Andalusia," she said.

We spoke about agriculture in Alentejo and the professor painted a picture of widespread agro-industry financed by foreign money, including Dutch and Spanish, practising monocultures and employing workers from countries like Nepal, Bangladesh, Ukraine and Brazil. She said the problem with this intensive agriculture, of olives, bamboo and other crops, was that it depleted soils after 10 years or so. She said there had been a long history of outsiders coming into Alentejo and transforming the landscape. The region is known for its extensive wheat fields.

Later in the conversation we returned to demographics, which was clearly a central concern for the professor. "We are few and old," she said of Portugal, adding after a silence of several seconds: "This is the drama."

Portugal's population, nearly 10.3 million in 2017, has fallen steadily since 2010 when it peaked at nearly 10.6 million. The country has one of the lowest fertility rates in the world and the Portuguese tend to attribute that to the financial struggle of bringing up a family. In the worst-case scenario, the National Statistics Institute says that the population could drop to 6.3 million by 2060. In a more upbeat central forecast, the institute expects the country to lose two million people over the next 40-odd years.

"We are few and old," does not have quite the ring of Henry V's "We few, we happy few, we band of brothers." But as a realistic summary of Portugal, away from the bustling cities of the coast, it is hard to beat.

CHAPTER 17

The Plains of Alentejo

Arrow-straight roads as far as the eye can see. Hours of walking time between villages. Setting out from Évora to Beja, some 78 kilometres to the south across the plains of Alentejo, I had one main thought – I need a policy on thinking as I tackle the journey ahead.

This is primarily a book on Portugal, of course. But it is also an account of a long-distance walk so I shall set Portugal aside for a moment and say something about my thoughts. I am no expert on meditation but I tried to use the idea of a walking meditation on gratitude. It more or less worked. I found that late in the day, when I was starting to look forward to that beer and wondering where I was going to lay my head, I didn't even try to do a walking meditation. It worked best in the morning and the early afternoon. I didn't have any big revelations, but the direction of my thoughts sometimes surprised me. I focused first on important people in my life and then on the small good deeds that people had done for me. I remembered a letter I received long ago from a Reuters colleague. I was taking over from him in the Bonn bureau and he wrote me a letter telling me, in positive terms, about my new colleagues and the city that would be my home. I remembered all of this clearly and it happened in 1977. "Gwnewch y pethau bychain," as St David said. Do the little things. They matter and people remember them long afterwards, with gratitude.

It took me three gratitude-filled days to reach Beja. On the second day, walking from Viana do Alentejo to Cuba, I was charmed to see several egrets moving imperiously across a field, from left to right, all standing on the backs of sheep. It was a little vignette of nature doing stand-up comedy and brought a smile to my face.

I reached Cuba after nightfall and asked a man and a woman walking their dog if they knew of any accommodation. We all walked together – they turned out be mother and son – and they bent their minds to the question. We did a mini-tour of Cuba and they showed me a statue. "That's Christopher Columbus," the woman said. "He was born here."

They decided the fire station would be a good bet and the son phoned the station commander whom he knew personally. He got the thumbs-up and off we went. There is a fine tradition in Portugal of fire stations providing accommodation for pilgrims, so their choice was not eccentric. At the fire station, a fireman told me that my lodgings for the night would be the women's bathroom, which I would have entirely to myself. He put two wooden benches in there and that was to be my bed. I sat down on a bench, got out some bread rolls and cheese and felt deeply content. I will remember the mother and son and Cuba fire station.

The next morning I went back to that statue. Christopher Columbus born in Alentejo? That certainly was the claim. An inscription on the statue said his real name was Salvador Fernandes Zarco, son of Fernando, Duke of Beja, and Isabel Goncalves Zarco. This was presented as HISTORICAL TRUTH (in big letters, in English and Portuguese) and as the conclusion of "remarkable historians and researchers".

I discovered that not only was there a statue, but a few metres away was the Cristovao Colon Centre, a small information office with panels and books, all dedicated to the proposition that the man was Portuguese. The theory was new to me but I quickly learned that it had surfaced in the 20th century and in the Portuguese-speaking world at least it had gained traction in recent years. In 2005 the Portuguese writer Jose Rodrigues Dos Santos published a best-selling novel, *Codex 632*, with a Portuguese Christopher Columbus as the central character.

There are several strands to the argument presented in Cuba. One element is that Salvador Fernandes Zarco was both illegitimate and partly Jewish since Isabel was of a Portuguese Jewish family from Tomar. Hence, in the social climate of the time, he had two hits against him, two reasons to keep his true origins secret.

The information centre puts a lot of focus on the names assigned to New World locations, to try to discredit the traditional view that the navigator was from a family of weavers in Genoa. One English-language panel says: "Cristovao Colon did not assign Italian names to the territories he has discovered; however about 40 place names are Portuguese, many of them from Alentejo.

"To the first discovered island he called San Salvador (his own name?), to the second island Santa Maria da Conceicao (Prince Fernando of Beja built a convent dedicated to her), to the third Fernandina (from the surname "Fernandes" son of Fernando?), to the fourth he put the name of Isabella (in honour of the Queen who hired him...or of his mother?), to the fifth island he called Cuba: name of a town in Alentejo..."

The mainstream view is that Cuba comes from a word in the now extinct Taino language, though the precise meaning of the word is not clear.

One intriguing element is the historical fact that when Christopher Columbus returned to Europe he landed first in Portugal and sought out the Portuguese king, John II, for a conversation. Only later did he proceed to Spain to brief the monarchs Ferdinand and Isabella, his patrons for the voyage.

So, a slice of travel! Sometimes travels provide answers, but often they raise new questions that one has never troubled to contemplate before. Few events in history have the resonance of that 1492 voyage across the Atlantic so I didn't want to kiss off that statue in Cuba with just one paragraph. But I can't give readers a definitive view on the real identity of Christopher Columbus. The majority opinion is that he came from Genoa, but there are many other theories. Indeed Portuguese writers alone have put forward two separate candidates. There is a view, embraced by amateur historian Fernando Branco, that Columbus was in fact Portuguese aristocrat Pedro Manuel de Ataíde. At the time of writing, the debate continues.

From Cuba I walked to Beja, Pax Julia in Roman times. It is a city full of history and yet another Portuguese example of beauty and decay side by side. The Saturday morning food market, just in front of Beja's magnificent medieval castle, was the very picture of civilised urban living. A few minutes' walk away, in the main square, were decrepit buildings straight out of a film noir. Many of the cobbled pedestrian streets near the square had a deadness about them and I sensed that many houses in them were empty. A waiter who served me coffee in the central square, the Praça da Republica, told me that many people had moved out of the centre of town into modern homes on the outskirts.

A deserted building opposite my hostel's front door in the old town was in the most lamentable state, with filthy outside walls, great chunks of plaster missing to reveal the stonework and plants growing through the structure. It was an eyesore and the man who checked me into the hostel viewed it with disgust.

Yet I liked Beja. It had character by the bucketload and the eating and drinking were good. The city's decay summoned up my sympathy. I almost wanted to hug Beja and make it better. I am sad about the state of so many Portuguese settlements. From one perspective, the country was very lucky in the 20th century. Peace reigned in mainland Portugal; there was no total war in its streets and its cities received no visits from either the Luftwaffe or the RAF. In other words it was neutral in the Second World War. Its historic towns and cities came through that terrible century of European conflict unscathed. Today, many are showing signs of wear and tear. Not Lisbon particularly, it's doing OK. But even Porto, despite its spectacular tourism boom, has quite a few derelict buildings in its core.

The decrepitude of so many Portuguese streets is not something the guidebooks stress, of course, because they are selling charm. But the gap between guidebookspeak and reality can be stark. I admire the Lonely Planet guides, but I do not agree with their description of Beja's main square as "renovated" and "attractive". The Praça da Republica looked awful. On the façade of one three-storey building great chunks of plaster had come away leaving bare masonry. It was urban decay writ large. Beja is in the poorest mainland province of Portugal, and Portugal is the poorest country in Western Europe. So the square is, if you like, one image of poverty in 21st century Europe. The waiter in the café explained to me that there had been renovation of the square's paving, but visitors to a city have a habit of looking up as well as down.

From Beja I continued my journey down through Alentejo. On the 54-kilometre stretch of road between Beja and Mértola there was, to the best of my knowledge, no accommodation at all. I was advised by locals to walk off the main road to a village called Alcaria Ruiva, which had a hotel. This meant at least a couple of hours walking in the dark. To my great happiness, on one stretch of my walk before I left the main road, I had the company of storks. For kilometre after kilometre they were nesting, mainly on a line of telegraph poles to the left of me. To be sociable, I shouted up to one stork: "Why do you prefer poles to trees?" The stork flew off and I got no answer to a perfectly reasonable question. On arrival at Alcaria Ruiva I discovered that the one small hotel was full but I eventually prevailed upon a restaurant-owner to provide me with a bed for the night.

The next day was a more modest walk, across delightful country. The flat plains were behind me now and I strolled through a landscape of hills and wooded valleys. In the early evening light I entered the medieval town of Mértola up on a hill. I had been greatly enjoying Alentejo but the best was still to come.

For weeks I had puzzled over the photo on the cover of my Michelin map of south Portugal. Where on earth was that beautiful place? The photo shows a winding river and to the right of it a little whitewashed tower with an outside staircase and a row of picturesque houses with orange tiled roofs, street lamps and balconies. It all looks so Portuguese, so inviting. In Mértola I strolled through the narrow streets, drinking it all in. "I've seen this place before," I thought. My mind slowly made the connection – it was Mértola on the cover of Michelin map 593. Mértola quickly became one of my favourite Portuguese towns. It has spirit, beauty. All it needs now is more people, to overcome the familiar challenge – the Grim Reaper working faster than the forces of rejuvenation.

My first thought when I saw Mértola and its imposing castle on the top of the hill was "North Africa, it looks like North Africa." For me, it had the jizz of a Maghreb settlement. As I got to know it better, my first impressions were borne out. This was a place that valued its links with the Muslim world.

On arrival I checked into a hostel on the other side of the Guadiana River from the town itself. From my dormitory window, the castle and the white houses beneath it filled the view. It was a cosy, distinctive hostel and a log fire burned in the lounge. An elderly receptionist, a woman from Lvov, checked me in. She

Mértola, one of my favourite Portuguese towns

struggled with the computer technology but chatted amiably in Ukrainian-accented Portuguese. She and her husband were the live-in custodians of the hostel and one evening the household echoed to the sound of Ukrainian as the couple phoned home.

I sank into the town as one does into a comfortable armchair. I was relaxed but also learning things. This is hunting country and on my first outing to a restaurant I learned a new word – *javali*, wild boar. This is such a fine spirited word for an untamed, tusked creature darting through the woods.

I dropped into an Islamic art museum and that's where I first discovered that Mértola consciously nourishes its cultural ties to North Africa. After all, Mértola was part of the Muslim world for centuries. In the art museum they showed a five-minute film, without commentary, which dwelt on the similarities between traditions in Portugal and Morocco. It was filmed in the Moroccan town of Chefchaouen, in the Rif Mountains, and locations in Portugal. It showed women tying headscarves and using henna, men building houses with adobe and ploughing with livestock.

At the castle and in the main church there are things that are very rare in Portugal. Just outside the castle walls there is an imposing statue of a 12th century poet and political leader, Ibn Qasi, who was briefly the governor of Mértola. He came from a rich Christian family and converted to Sufism. I had not seen any other statues of Muslims in Portugal.

After the castle I went to the church which has within it significant parts of a 12th century mosque. The visitor can see original Moorish arches and, behind the altar, what was a Muslim mihrab or prayer niche. Portuguese Christian knights conquered Mértola from the Moors in 1238. At the church, a caretaker/guide told me that the Christians simply had no money to finance the mosque's demolition so it remained standing. Later it was converted to a church.

To learn about Mértola's present, I had a conversation with the president of the municipal chamber, a Socialist Party politician called Jorge Rosa. He received me at his office, with views over a little square filled with orange trees. Rosa embodied cautious optimism and never once was his tone one of complaint. He had a more modest role than Barack Obama, of course, but I felt that like Obama he understood that politicians needed to take a long view – in the arc of history there will be hard times, there will be reverses.

I asked Rosa what he saw as Mértola's biggest challenge. "Population," he said without any hesitation. He told me that for every 100 deaths in the municipality, between 25 and 30 children were born. I discovered in Portugal that the good professionals, be it in politics, academia or journalism, had the local population figures at their fingertips.

Rosa said the population of the municipality – the town and surrounding countryside – had fallen from some 18,000 half a century ago to about 7,000 today. The population of the town itself had dropped from about 2,000 to 1,600. Mechanisation of agriculture, he said, had fuelled an exodus from the countryside in the late 20th century. One big event that drove thousands from this part of Portugal was the closure of a British-owned copper mine in Mina de São Domingos in 1966.

"This mine used to employ 4,000 to 5,000 people," Rosa said, adding that with miners' families included it supported about 15,000 people.

Rosa highlighted the demographic strangeness of today's Portugal, with so many people living in the western half. "Portugal is a country that has 10 million inhabitants," he said. "From north to south one half of the country has one million or less and the other half has nine million. It is an immense imbalance."

Mértola, he said, had five inhabitants per square kilometre, making it one of the emptiest parts of Portugal. For an international comparison, this is a lower population density than the Highlands of Scotland.

"We are feeling a lack of manpower, people to work," he said. "We are having recourse to a lot of foreign manpower, mainly for agriculture. Romanians, Spaniards, Asians…"

One thread in our conversation was the arrival in Mértola of outsiders who were bringing not muscle power but new ideas. Rosa brought up the name of Ernst Götsch, a Swiss farmer and researcher known internationally for his pioneering work in Brazil bringing degraded land back into productive use. He said that a Brazilian couple were seeking to use Götsch's methods of agroforestry in Mértola. He cited other "adventurous people" who were coming to the region.

He gave a historical dimension to the region's challenges and argued that the worst periods were long past. One difficult period for Mértola, he said, was the 1970s. In the middle of this decade, in 1974, Portugal had a revolution that ended a long period of authoritarian rule. It was an edgy time. "From 1970 to 1980 people lived very badly in the municipality. It was a period when the municipality didn't really develop."

The turnaround had been since the start of the new millennium. "The last 20 years have been very important for Mértola," he said. "In the last 20 years we have seen the development of tourism." He stressed the role of archaeology in uncovering the town's history, providing more information on the periods of Roman and Islamic rule. Nature tourism had grown – the region is a habitat for the critically endangered Iberian lynx and the species is being re-introduced to the Guadiana valley from Spain. The town was making better use of the river, he said, and I had seen plenty of people out kayaking.

Rosa, who had been elected to his post three times, expressed optimism that Mértola would succeed in attracting back some of the young people who had left. He highlighted tourism and organic farming as two sectors that would be pivotal for Mértola's future.

It was Rosa's job to boost Mértola, but I left his office feeling that here was a man who was both rooted in his region and open to foreign ideas. I experienced it as a heartening conversation. He did not hide the toughness of Mértola's summer temperatures that could, he said, go up to 47C. But perhaps the most effective salesman is an honest one.

In Mértola I went into one other office, an estate agent, to ask about the local property market. Where was interest coming from? A man and a woman working there gave me an impressive list of countries. The man leafed through his correspondence file. Their list was Belgium, the Netherlands, Austria, Brazil, Spain, Canada, Australia, France, Germany, Luxembourg, Italy, Denmark and Britain. The French, Spanish and Dutch predominated. And what would I get for 100,000 euros? The answer was a big house, with four or five bedrooms, and a large garden. But they had many properties for far less. A Dutchman had just bought a two-bedroom house in the village of São Sebastião dos Carros for 15,000 euros.

If buying foreign property is not for you but you are curious to see Mértola, every two years the town hosts an Islamic festival. The last one had been disrupted by a strong gale, but organisers hoped for more clement weather when the next edition took place in May 2019. Some of the town's streets would be converted into a souk and the town would give full voice to the Islamic side of its history and traditions.

CHAPTER 18

Thoughts from the Algarve

I walked across the Algarve from east to west, from the Spanish border to the Atlantic, travelling about 300 kilometres. It was a rich experience, triggering thoughts on a range of subjects. The diverse musings all sprang organically from my travels in these parts. Topics included the goals of Iberian federalism and the perils of impatience, the genius of Moorish engineering and the curves of a Hollywood legend. The cultural backdrop to the whole Algarve walk was the changing dynamics from the sleepy hamlets of the depopulated east to the cosmopolitan beat of the more prosperous west.

For a north European, the very word Algarve has powerful connotations of the sun-kissed south. But the word actually comes from the Arabic for the west, *al-Gharb*. From the perspective of the Arab rulers who had control of most of the Iberian Peninsula from the eighth century, the Algarve was a western part of their domains. So the word is a living verbal remnant from the geopolitics of a forgotten world.

From Mértola I walked south to the Algarve town of Alcoutim. Crossing a stream into the Algarve I noted one immediate change – the decoration of the houses. The signature colours of Alentejo dwellings are white and blue and this gives a distinct character to the great region that makes up about a third of Portugal. When

I reached the Algarve the first two houses I saw were quite different; one was pink and the other yellow. I had moved on.

Mértola to Alcoutim was one of the longest days of my Portugal walk. I covered about 42 kilometres, the distance of the Marathon. Alcoutim is the most sparsely populated municipality in Portugal and there was nowhere to stay along the route unless I camped. After nightfall I kept marching on for several hours buoyed by news on my mobile phone that Wales had beaten England at rugby. Alcoutim seemed dead when I arrived, but I chanced upon an Irishman and croaked out "Where can a man get a drink in this town?" He pointed me in the right direction and I slaked a Marathon-sized thirst with beer.

Alcoutim, like Mértola, is on the Guadiana River and on the other side of the river is Spain. There is no bridge across the river here and no car ferry either. I took a little passenger boat over to the small Spanish town of Sanlucar de Guadiana for Sunday lunch, looking for telltale cultural differences between Portugal and Spain. I didn't find a whole lot. Both towns were clusters of white houses with red roofs and both had castles facing the traditional foe on the other side of the river. Yet the two towns definitely felt different, in ways that were hard to define. The Spanish bar where I ate offered fresh orange juice and I reflected that cafés in Portugal, although there are orange trees galore, often don't sell the fresh juice. This is not a huge cultural divide.

On the surface, the absence of a bridge fitted with the conventional idea of Spain and Portugal having a "back-to-back" relationship, living side by side but with minimal interaction. But even on a short visit to Alcoutim it became clear the truth was more complex. A sign in the central square of Alcoutim gave an account of the town's history and made a point of saying it was "a strong wish of the people in both towns" to have a bridge. The town also had big signs advertising an arts festival planned for March that it organised in collaboration with Sanlucar de Guadiana. In a nod to the venerable tradition of cross-border smuggling in this region, the event is called the Festival do Contrabando, with the tongue in cheek tag of "arts trafficking on the Guadiana".

Being on the border prompted me to delve a little into how Spain and Portugal viewed one another. Because Portugal often fought against its neighbour, its relationship with Spain can be prickly. Whereas the Vatican recognised Portugal's independence in a papal Bull of 1179, Spain's blessing came nearly five centuries later, in 1668. Both countries are now members of the European Union and the depth of hostility that once existed has gone. But there is still an edge. Individual Portuguese can be positively rude about the Spanish.

But since relationships are complex, this is just one facet of a many-sided tale. There has been a thread in Spanish intellectual life of stressing the importance for the Spanish of understanding Portugal, its language, its literature and its history. In 20th century Spain, Miguel de Unamuno was probably the leading voice giving this message to his compatriots. Unamuno, a Basque writer and twice rector of the University of Salamanca, gave his support to the cause of Iberian federalism.

An opinion poll conducted by the University of Salamanca in 2011 found that nearly 40 percent of Spaniards and 46 percent of Portuguese supported a federation. But it's not a live political issue and a union of Spain and Portugal is not an imminent event.

Transport links between the two countries are not exactly state-of-the-art. For decades there has been talk of a high-speed train between Lisbon and Madrid but the Portuguese government pulled out of a project to make this happen back in 2012, citing the high financial cost. So the night train from Lisbon to Madrid (there are daytime options too) takes 10 hours 10 minutes to cover about 500 kilometres. The Portuguese government has made clear that its priority is not a Lisbon-Madrid high-speed line at all, but improving train links along the Atlantic coast, from Lisbon via Porto to Vigo. Now Vigo is in Galicia, the part of Spain that is linguistically and culturally closest to Portugal.

In the 20th century, it could be argued that Portugal did well to keep a political distance from Spain. When Spain descended into the savagery of civil war in 1936, atrocities unfolded right on Portugal's doorstep. I am thinking in particular of the mass killings carried out by Nationalist forces – the side led by General Francisco Franco – in the bullring of the Spanish city of Badajoz in August 1936.

But in Portugal the ripples from this horrific bloodletting in Spain were modest. The worst that happened was a small anti-Salazar naval mutiny in Lisbon in September 1936 when 12 Portuguese sailors died.

In the 21st century, when both countries have restored democracy and joined the European Union, a federation could perhaps make sense. Certainly the Portuguese writer José Saramago, whose name has already appeared on these pages, believed that Portugal's future lay in an Iberian union. "It is inevitable that we will end up joining with Spain," he said late in his life, to the annoyance of some of his compatriots. Saramago walked the Iberian federalist talk by marrying Spanish journalist Pilar del Rio, who became a Portuguese citizen.

I played with the whole federation idea in my head. In the age of Brexit, a move away from narrow nationalism could be a refreshing change for Europe. A union of Spain and Portugal would need a capital, of course, and why not build a new capital on both sides of the Guadiana River? This would avoid the difficult conversation of whether to choose Madrid or Lisbon. A new capital on the Guadiana could provide a much-needed impetus to the economy in the border regions of Spain and Portugal, both beset by a critical lack of people. Beyond the suburbs of the new capital the Iberian lynx would roam wild and the city would be a plum posting for nature-loving diplomats.

There is just one problem with this romantic vision. Regardless of the University of Salamanca opinion poll, it has been impossible in my experience to encounter any Portuguese in favour of an Iberian union. I have not met a single one. When I have raised the subject with Portuguese people, the reaction has always been a distinct impatience with the very suggestion. So as a visitor, trying to be sensitive to local feelings, I have let the question drop.

What has changed immensely in recent decades is the amount of trade between the two countries. Portugal and Spain joined what was then the European Economic Community on the same day, 12 June 1985. Before then, trade between the two was minimal, but after their accession to the bloc Spain quickly became Portugal's biggest trade partner.

From Alcoutim, my plan was to walk along the Via Algarviana, a long-distance path that crosses the Algarve following a meandering inland route through hilly country. The beginning of the path was delightful, with the winding Guadiana in full view on my right. I walked past gnarled olive trees and a whimsical sign in English announcing Upper Hill Farm. But the path kept heading northwest when the ultimate destination on day one lay southwest of Alcoutim. I grew impatient and in the village of Cortes Pereiras – which I had walked through two days earlier on my way south – I sought an alternative route. I met a retired policeman in a café and he showed me a dirt track to the village of Corte Tabelião that was shorter than the waymarked Via Algarviana. He cautioned that the route was very hilly.

The retired policeman did not literally say "You can't go wrong" but he offered his advice in that spirit. I set out and you will probably not be surprised that I never set eyes on Corte Tabelião. I quickly discovered that the Algarve was indeed very different from the flat plains of Alentejo. The Algarve has ravines. It also has thorn bushes and rocks and it takes great delight in putting these in close proximity to one another in said ravines. I am sure you get the picture. Suffice it to say that at five in the afternoon I was back in the café where I had stopped four hours earlier, this time with knees punctured by thorns and a profoundly bruised ego. I can only conclude that a combination of poor navigation skills and impatience is dangerous. "Don't do stupid things," is probably a fair summary of my learning. After this débacle I had a forced march on roads and eventually made it to my B&B late in the evening.

On the following days I scrupulously avoided any unneeded adventures and I stuck to either the Via Algarviana or metalled roads. The highlight on day two was fording the Foupana River. This was not a raging torrent, but it required a little sit-down and some quiet thought. In the end I walked through with boots on and trousers rolled up, once with my backpack and a second time carrying a plastic bag with food.

I reached Furnazinhas, a sleepy one-donkey Algarve village, without mishap and checked into a little B&B, the Casa do Lavrador, managed by a couple in their thirties from Lisbon, Ricardo and Carolina Romero. On my arrival Carolina offered me a fresh orange juice, demolishing the thought I'd entertained two days earlier on a supposed cultural difference between Portugal and Spain.

Carolina, Ricardo and their young son Alexandre, who was nearly two when I stayed with them, are an outpost of what the Portuguese describe as *os novos rurais*, the new rural people who have exchanged the big city for what the British call the good life in the country. In the hills of the eastern Algarve, it takes pluck for a young family to opt for the good life. The practical difficulties are daunting. For a supermarket shop, the Romeros face a 60-kilometre round trip to the coast. When young Alexandre reaches school age they will have to do nearly 70 kilometres of driving every day. There will be no school bus, no government help of any kind. Alexandre is a full half-century younger than the youngest established villager, who is 52. No playmates in the village for him.

I talked to the couple about their new life, which had begun just a few months earlier. What were their biggest challenges? "Contact with people," said Carolina. "We're not from here. It's not very easy." Ricardo explored the business dimension. He said on average one walker a day stayed with them. To be sustainable, the little business they managed had to have other strings to its bow. They were looking at a range of other possible activities to attract holidaymakers – birdwatching, yoga and classes on weaving and making rope from cacti. These are traditional local crafts and Ricardo said classes could do the two jobs of generating income and involving village people.

If you're ever walking the Via Algarviana, I warmly recommend the Casa do Lavrador. They served me the best salad I ate in Portugal and they're trying to keep a village alive.

After Furnazinhas I spent two more days sticking mainly to the Via Algarviana. On the eastern stretches of this path, both the Chief Financial Officer and the Commissariat Department in any expedition have to stay awake. All the B&Bs wanted cash and after leaving Alcoutim there was no ATM until the end of day four, in the village of Cachopo. There were very few restaurants or shops and I found it best to book dinner ahead in the next night's accommodation. I took the remains of breakfast as my picnic lunch. The website viaalgarviana.org is the essential source of information and it has downloadable maps of the path.

By the time I reached Cachopo, I was conscious of a serious drop in my energy levels. And what's the use of a low-energy travel writer? There was no mystery about the reasons. By the time I started on the Via Algarviana I had already walked more than 1,100 kilometres. I wasn't in the right frame of mind for a long-distance path. Even vagrants can get set in their habits and I was used to café stops to break the day's walk. I enjoyed the occasional "bom dia" from a woman on a balcony. The red-earth Via Algarviana, threading its way endlessly, up and down, up and down, sometimes through pine plantations, was just too lonely. It sapped my spirit. I looked at the idea of dropping down to the coast, but settled for the option of staying inland, following the general route of the path but on roads. This worked and my energies revived.

I had no regrets about following an inland route, away from the resorts of the Algarve coast so familiar to millions of north European visitors. I was able to see that rural life does still include traditional activities. Every day I saw active beehives, even in remote places. In the villages I sometimes passed great piles of harvested cork bark.

This is, of course, one man's subjective account, but I felt that I walked out of the sleepy eastern hills of the Algarve and into the more cosmopolitan west in the village of Barranco do Velho. There is nothing remarkable about this place but it is on National Route 2, the famous north-south road that I have mentioned before. Suddenly the language changed. I walked into my hotel and the receptionist greeted me in English. In the restaurant at dinner, English was the only language spoken. The food changed. It became what I think of as tourist food, perfectly OK but probably no more Portuguese than roast beef and Yorkshire pudding. I ate prawns, artistically arranged on a bed of bananas, kiwi and other fruit.

From Barranco do Velho onwards the houses looked bigger and so did the cars. The dogs still came in all shapes and sizes, but their bark seemed a tad more insistent. They certainly had more stuff to guard.

My route to the west took me just north of the village of Salir. I walked through alluring countryside, with bright orange flowers by the roadside. Beyond the flowers, on my right, were scattered homes and then a glorious limestone massif, the Rocha da Pena, a rocky plateau about two kilometres long. As a Welshman, I like a good upland and the Rocha da Pena, reaching 480 metres in altitude, was a most welcome sight. On top of the massif are two stone walls that might date back to the Iron Age. Moors fleeing from the military advances of King Dom Afonso III took refuge in these defences in the 13th century. It was Dom Afonso (1210-1279) who conquered the Algarve and made it part of the Portuguese kingdom.

Linguistically, from this day onwards I felt that I was walking through a Portuguese-English condominium. This was strange at first.

"Marcia, get in the middle." The peremptory command of a mother, uttered in your own mother tongue in a foreign land, can have the most riveting force. These banal words, spoken in the village of Alte as an English family climbed into their car, constitute one strong memory from the day I walked to Alte from Barranco do Velho. For most of my rural wanderings in Portugal, I had seldom heard English spoken by a native.

The next day, so on day eight of my Algarve walk, I reached Silves, the first place of any real size I had seen since Beja. I walked in at night, drawn by the city's magnificent medieval castle on a hill. Portugal has so many castles, but I never grew tired of them. Silves castle has a singular history. The Moors occupied Silves for more than four centuries but a force of Crusaders, which included English knights, took the castle after a three-month siege in 1189. The Moors surrendered because they ran out of water. Two years

147

later, they took back the castle and held it for the next 60 years. In that time they built an extraordinary water supply system for the castle. According to the official Silves literature on the fortification, this system had an estimated capacity of 1.3 million litres that meant it could supply about 1,200 people for nearly a year. To my amazement, it supplied Silves with water until the 1990s. I had no idea before that Moorish engineering had provided a Portuguese city with an essential part of its infrastructure until the late 20th century.

Back in the Moorish period, Silves was an important centre of Arabic culture. It was known for the elegance of its spoken Arabic and earned the nickname "the Baghdad of the West". Its golden age was the 11th century when it was called Xelb. A city of rose gardens and palaces, it drew scholars and artists from distant parts of the Islamic world. Xelb's crowning architectural glory was the Palace of the Verandas, venue for royal banquets and concerts.

Silves draws tourists from all over Europe. One newsagent offered Bild, the Daily Mail, even Russia's Dokumenti I Fakti. I stayed in a hostel in a brilliant location, just a few metres from a Roman bridge over the Arade river. It stood inside its own orange orchard. Silves has the reputation of producing the country's best, sweetest oranges.

The owner, Helena, plied me with local tales. Everyone in the tourism business likes a little bit of stardust sprinkled on their patch and she told me that back in the 1960s Ingrid Bergman was a visitor to Silves. On one of her visits to Portugal, in 1963, the star of *Casablanca* was fined for wearing too skimpy a bikini on an Algarve beach. It is a news story from another age.

CHAPTER 19

The Sea, the Sea

From Silves onwards I felt on the home straight. True, it was actually a long and winding home straight, going north at first, then west and finally south. But surely not more than a week's walking lay ahead of me and the thought of reaching the sea drew me on.

I got ready to return to the Via Algarviana, for a long one-day hike to Monchique up through hilly country. I had the path downloaded onto my phone. But just before I set out, Helena, the hostel owner, counselled against it. She said week-long wildfires that had raged between Silves and Monchique in August 2018 had destroyed the waymarks and one walker had recently got lost on the route. I followed her advice and kept to the road.

It rained for much of the walk, but storks north of the town of Porto de Lagos brightened my day. I passed many dozens of storks, nesting on telegraph poles, lampposts, trees, bushes and a big derelict building. I know I go on about storks when I see them, but they transform a landscape. Like swans, they manage to be both big and elegant. They are a presence in the land, both because of their looks but also on account of their bill-clattering. This sounds like a muffled jackhammer and is unlike any other sound I have heard in nature. The stork makes the sound by quickly opening and shutting its beak and a throat pouch apparently amplifies the noise. The purpose of the behaviour can be to sound an alarm or just to communicate a greeting. Sometimes I have heard storks first and then looked up to see them perched high above me.

The road climbed and, after nightfall, up in the hills I walked through the spa town of Caldas de Monchique, once favoured by Portuguese monarchs. Even after dark the town's cobbled streets had charm and serenity. Perhaps like all the best spas it had an aura of faded elegance.

The next day, heading from Monchique to Marmelete over to the west, I passed through country of spellbinding beauty, green wooded hills with white red-roofed houses dotted around a valley. There were groves full of birdsong, citrus orchards with oranges and lemons, camellias, cork oak trees and well-kept houses with colourful gardens.

After the village of Casais, way off to my left, about 18 kilometres to the south, there was something I couldn't positively identify. An old man wearing a cap and carrying garden tools crossed the road just ahead of me. I greeted him and asked: "Excuse me, is that a mist or the sea?" "That is the sea," he said.

It was a sweet Xenophon moment. Thalassa, thalassa! The sea, the sea. Portugal's destiny has been so bound up with the sea that my mainly inland route could be considered eccentric. I had wanted to travel through lesser-known parts of the country, well away from the popular seaside resorts. But I had become very aware that I needed to redress the balance. Finally, for the first time since Lisbon, I rested my eyes upon the ocean. It was an emotional moment; I was connecting with one very important aspect of what for me had become a beloved country.

On my second day out of Silves, I made it to Aljezur, a picturesque town a few kilometres inland that is particularly popular with Germans. In our present age, when the world takes a shine to a place there is a certain predictability about what comes next.

True to form, Aljezur has its funky vegan café, set in a converted flourmill. It has ads for yoga, Reiki retreats and reassuringly expensive fish restaurants. But hey, this is all so much better than dying villages.

Out one day in Aljezur, I asked an elderly man walking with a stick for directions. He replied in English to my Portuguese-language question and we struck up a conversation. Friedrich Germann was his name and in no time at all he gave me his life story. He told me that he spoke Swiss German, English, Italian, Norwegian, Swedish, Danish and some Spanish, but during his long retirement in Portugal he had felt no need to learn Portuguese. He had many Scandinavian friends living in the nearby countryside and he could talk to them in their own languages.

He had started his working life as a mess boy on freighters. He had also been a dairy farmer in his native Switzerland and later a captain of cruise liners. He travelled the world on ships, from French Polynesia to the Caribbean. He met his second wife, Maria from the United States, when she was a passenger aboard one of his cruise ships. They had both been living in Aljezur for 16 years and I have never seen a happier man.

He retired at the age of 63. He recounted how he came to choose Portugal as his home and recalled a day in Norway. "I was listening to the radio and there was this lovely-speaking Norwegian woman who had travelled the world. 'If you want to retire you have to go to Portugal because the weather is beautiful and no pollution, no industry…It is laid back.' Ah, that is where I want to live!"

Having selected Portugal for retirement, how did he pick Aljezur? "I bought a, what do you call it, mobile home in Germany, near Frankfurt, unseen, on the net…I drove through France, Spain, over to north Portugal. I had already found a real estate agent."

He went to Coimbra. "I didn't like it. Coimbra as a city, yes, but the mountains there are very wet. Everything was moss, every tree, every stone, everything was full of moss. It was not for me." So, on the advice of the estate agents he and his wife headed further south, looking for somewhere high up with a fine view and good air.

One day they drove south from the nearby village of Rogil and for the first time they saw Aljezur, with its 10th century Moorish castle perched above the town. As they sat in their vehicle Germann knew at once that he had found his soul place.

"I saw this beautiful castle and white buildings, like a little village. I said to my wife 'Maria, oh that is where I want, that is exactly where I want to live." Pointing up the hill, towards Aljezur castle, he said to me: "So here is the castle and behind the bend here is my house." Then he dissolved into a wonderful laugh of deep contentment.

He had suffered a stroke in Portugal, which robbed him of his ability to drive. "But I am still going strong," he said and I didn't doubt him. This conversation with an exultant 80-year-old was one of the memorable encounters of my walk. Portugal has found an honourable vocation, making retired foreigners happy.

The next day too proved exceptional. I walked west from Aljezur to the ruins of a 12th century Sufi fortress-monastery, on a little promontory called Ponta da Atalaia with cliffs on three sides and the Atlantic rolling in. This lonely place is the Ribat of Arrifana. Its founder was the Sufi Master Ibn Qasi, whose statue stands in Mértola.

It was built around 1130, but Muslim assassins killed Ibn Qasi in Silves in 1151 and the whole complex fell into decay. Eight-and-a-half centuries passed before archaeologists Mário and Rosa Varela Gomes identified this site as the long-lost Ribat of Arrifana in 2001. (*Ribat* is an Arabic word meaning fortification.) They found the remains of nine mosques on the site and they believe that this was the capital of a theocratic state that briefly covered the whole south of present-day Portugal and part of western Andalusia.

There is no signage telling you how to find this place and once you've arrived there is nothing telling you what you are looking at. The ruins are modest, essentially the remains of walls, just a few stones high. But this is a unique place, a former Sufi citadel on West European soil. I sat on a Sufi stone for my picnic lunch, facing northeast to watch the waves breaking on the Atlantic shore. A few visitors trickled in, but not enough to disturb the calm. This still feels like a holy place, with earth, air and water all present in celebration of the Sufi principle of Divine oneness.

Ibn Qasi, who was from an ancient and wealthy Christian family, turned to Sufism and became a significant figure in the complex geopolitics of his day. He was a thinker and a writer and historians believe that he probably wrote his religious treatise *The Removal of the Sandals* at the ribat he established. He also became a political leader, allied to Afonso Henriques, Portugal's first king. In the 1140s he led a major revolt against the Muslim Almoravid Empire. The Almoravids, with their capital in Marrakesh, ruled from what is now Spain in the north to present-day Mauritania in the south. Ibn Qasi's murder seems to have been the work of Muslims angered by his alliance with a Christian king.

I had come to the promontory mainly along an inland route, but on my return I started by walking north on a clifftop path, with ocellated lizards scuttling in the sand at my feet. The path emerged at the beautiful bay of Monte Clerigo and from there it was a gentle walk on roads and woodland paths back to Aljezur.

Two days later I left Aljezur, walking south by road as far as Bensafrim. The next day, finally, I returned to the Via Algarviana, for a stroll of just seven kilometres to Barão de São João. It was a world away from the Via Algarviana over in the east. It had people! I exchanged a few words with a young Portuguese man tending his vegetables. I encountered two young English girls on bicycles and one gaily tossed a "boa tarde" in my direction. I walked through entrancing cork oak woodland and then met a woman gardener, at work right by the path. Her name was Angie and she had moved from northeast England to the Algarve. She was a painter and appreciated what the Algarve had to offer. "The light here is just fantastic," she said. She had an exhibition of her work running in the neighbourhood and like Friedrich Germann she radiated deep happiness.

I had heard from a friend that in Barão de São João there was a small organic food enterprise that planted heritage grains and baked organic bread. I wanted to learn more. In the village I quickly picked up its cosmopolitan, alternative vibe. In the Caramba bar, clocks on the wall claimed to give the time in Antananarivo (Madagascar) and Kiribati in the Pacific. The barmaid spoke German and served me a Dutch beer laced with Tequila. Outside in the street a group of French speakers sat around a woman cradling a guitar. I seemed on occasions to be one of the few men in town who did not have his hair tied at the back of his head in a bun. At my accommodation, my Portuguese host told me that the main language spoken in Barão de São João was English.

With the help of my host, I met up with Sandra Santos, a Portuguese anthropology graduate in her thirties who had set up the permaculture, food and arts initiative called Kultivarte. We met first in its shop and then went out to the back to see an area that served both as social hub and a small arts venue. Sandra explained what the group had been doing. On a two-hectare plot, they followed the principles of permaculture, a set of guidelines based on whole systems thinking. Sandra initiated me into the pleasure of drinking kombucha, a fizzy fermented drink that tasted extraordinary. Over the kombucha, she talked of her project.

"We grow organic ancient varieties of wheat and rye and then we have our own stone mill," she said. "We grind the cereals there, we make the flour in the moment. I do natural fermentation with mother dough. I make the dough by hand and it is baked in the wood oven. So we do organic, artisanal bread, trying to close all the cycle, cultivation to the final product."

With their vegetable garden, they followed the same principles. "We process our own vegetables and we create sauerkraut, zucchini jam, baba ganoush, so different processed and also fermented foods…We sell every Saturday in the local market."

Kultivarte opened in June 2018 and in March 2019 Sandra was seeking funding to establish it as a community-supported agriculture project and a community-supported bakery, accompanied by cultural and artistic activities. It was a joy to talk to the young Portuguese founder of an agricultural project, but I heard from Sandra a few months later that the project had not prospered. Their well had run dry.

I had picked up when I was in Barão de São João that water was a concern. People talked about a local water-guzzling avocado farm of 200 hectares. I read later in a Reuters report on the Algarve's avocado boom that this particular plantation used 3.5-4.1 million litres of water per day, according to the season. The attraction for the region's 110 growers is that they can sell avocados for an average of 2.20 euros per kilo, while oranges fetch only about 0.50 euros. But drought in the Algarve is now so severe that environmental groups are calling for a halt to further expansion of avocado production.

Another modern phenomenon in the Algarve, golfing, is also using precious water resources. A 2014 study by Professor Celestina Pedras from the University of the Algarve found that the region's 40 golf courses were being irrigated with some 18 million cubic metres of water a year. That represents more than 700mm of rain, while the Algarve capital Faro receives only about 500mm of rain per year.

CHAPTER 20

A Walk to the End of the World

Cape St Vincent in my sights, on the final day of the walk

To the chatter of birds in eucalyptus trees, past cacti, rich red earth and bonnie crops of beans, I set out to walk to the end of the world.

"I am walking to Sagres." That had been my mantra since the early days of this odyssey back in September 2018. Now, on 14 March 2019, I truly was walking to Sagres. It was hard to believe.

I started out from the inland town of Vila do Bispo, in the middle of a promontory with the sea on three sides. I took the scenic walk, via Cape St Vincent. For Europeans, this was for a very long time the end of the known world and this coast still has a wild, rugged feel. The south-western tip of the Algarve is generally regarded as one of the least spoiled coastlines of southern Europe.

From Vila do Bispo I followed a 14-kilometre waymarked route to the cape, walking first on a farmland track westward to the ocean. After a while the farmland ended and the track became a path, weaving its way southwest along the clifftops through a mosaic of plants. I walked now with deep blue sea to my right and straight ahead of me. With Sagres and the ocean as a backdrop, I watched a hawk hover and dive, once, twice, three times.

The flowering plants were a delight, fragrant and exotic. One common plant here is the Sagres gum rockrose. The different types of gum rockrose are covered with a sticky resin, which is the source of labdanum, used historically in herbal medicine (not to be confused with laudanum, the tincture of opium).

I saw more hikers on this final day of my journey than I had seen on the whole of the rest of my Portugal walk, but the numbers were still modest compared with the hordes that sometimes visit Welsh beauty spots. For most of the time, as Cape St Vincent slowly drew closer, I could see no one at all. The path, with its sea views, twists and turns and exuberant plant life, was quite the loveliest I had walked on in Portugal.

As a bonus, there were echoes of naval history. Over the centuries a number of battles have stained the seas off Cape St Vincent. The most famous was fought in 1797 between British and Spanish fleets, part of the French Revolutionary Wars. The British defeated a bigger Spanish force that included the *Santísima Trinidad*, the largest warship in the world. The British commander,

Sir John Jervis, ordered his ships to sail between two groups of Spanish ships and then engage them separately. The battle proved important in the rise of the fiercely ambitious Horatio Nelson, commander of the *Captain*. Nelson, fearing that several Spanish ships would escape unscathed, took his vessel out of the British line and offered himself to attack by seven enemy ships. Three British ships went to support him. Nelson drew the *Captain,* by now virtually disabled by enemy broadsides, alongside the nearest Spanish ship, the *San Nicolas.* Drawn sword in hand, Nelson led a boarding party and after capture of the *San Nicolas,* now in flames, used it as a bridge to seize the *San Jose* as well. Shortly after the battle, Nelson won promotion to rear admiral.

Today these waters are busy shipping lanes and the lighthouse at Cape St Vincent is one of the most powerful in Europe. Gastronomically, this little corner of Europe feels more like the north than the south. A bratwurst stand near the lighthouse offers certificates to customers who have bought their product, billed as the "letzte Bratwurst vor Amerika", the last bratwurst before America.

From Cape St Vincent it is about six kilometres to Sagres and the coastline here, with marshes, cliffs, dunes and lagoons, is a protected reserve. According to the website algarve-portal. com: "The Sagres Biogenetic Reserve is the only place in the world where white storks build their nests on sea cliffs and the only place in the country where there is a colony of otters using the marine environment to search for their food."

In the autumn, in this part of the south-western Algarve, thousands of migrating birds arrive. The visitors include sparrowhawks, honey buzzards, booted eagles, short-toed eagles, griffon vultures and Egyptian vultures.

Sagres itself is a holiday town, with an attractive harbour, restaurants galore, accommodation and surf hire shops. In tourist literature, much is made of the role of Sagres in Portugal's Age of Discoveries. Much of this story, it turns out, has no foundation. The central figure in the tale is always Prince Henry the Navigator. (The epithet Navigator, applied by the English, seldom by the Portuguese, is a misnomer since he never sailed on any exploratory voyage.)

Henry was governor of the Algarve and a wealthy man – he had Crown monopolies on trade with the Guinea coast of Africa, on tuna fishing in the Algarve, the importation of sugar and dyes and control of Portugal's soap industry. His power as monopolist prompted many protests over the years but it gave him considerable financial clout. Helped also by funds from the Order of Christ, which he headed, Henry was the most important patron of early African voyages. But in recent decades historians have considerably modified the picture of a heroic figure blazing a trail with modern scientific ideas.

A.R. Disney, in the second volume of his book *A History of Portugal and the Portuguese Empire,* wrote: "He emphatically did not set up an astronomical observatory at Sagres in the Algarve, as used to be thought, nor did he establish a 'school' to teach mathematics and astronomy to his navigators." Disney depicts Henry as a man obsessed with the religious struggle against Islam, whose main intellectual interest was theology. He was also very focused on winning the Canary Islands for Portugal, but those plans came to naught. It was the Castilians who won the Canaries. After Henry's death in 1460, the pace of Portuguese exploration in Africa actually quickened considerably.

The legend was that Henry's school of navigation was inside Sagres fort, which stands at the beginning of the Ponta de Sagres, a dramatic promontory with cliffs on three sides. The fort was attacked by Sir Francis Drake in 1587, the year when he also sailed into Cadiz harbour "to singe the beard" of the king of Spain.

When I visited, there were dozens of fishermen along the clifftops beyond the fort, cheerfully ignoring the warning signs not to approach the crumbling edge. They all stood beyond the signs, just above a precipitous drop, hoping to catch sea bream and bass. It was a potent final image of Portugal's intimate embrace of the sea.

Journey's end. From the Spanish town of Puebla de Sanabria to Sagres, I had followed a distinctly zigzag route and walked about 1,470 kilometres. This is further than the distance from Land's End to John o'Groats, the two extremities of the United Kingdom. I had been blessed with good health, with never a sign of a single blister.

A long solo walk is much more than an extended version of a day's or a week's hike. It is a profound intellectual and emotional experience as you learn both about the country where you are walking and about yourself. When I arrived at Sagres, shortly before my 69th birthday, I did have a sense of achievement, but I had no strong feeling of a journey ending. What emerged gradually, during the weeks after the end of the walk, was a profound sense of a new life chapter beginning.

Postscript: Dispatches from the Plague Year

Back in Wales I became restless again and my thoughts converged on one question: how about emigrating to Portugal? A sense that my future lay there grew stronger. Portugal sat more comfortably with me than the deeply riven United Kingdom. The two countries both had imperial histories, but in the post-imperial present they embraced different values. I liked the fact that Portugal had wolves and lynx roaming wild and no nuclear weapons or power stations. The UK, on the other hand, had both a nuclear armoury and nuclear power but no wolves and no lynx. Portugal somehow felt more at ease with itself than Brexit Blighty. Then there was the little matter of the radiant blue skies and the longer days in winter.

Friends expressed varying views on my proposed departure but my daughters were wholeheartedly supportive. Nine months after ending my walk I was back in Portugal. I spent Christmas with my daughters in England and then flew to Faro. Little did I know, of course, that a challenging time for the world lay just around the corner.

Living in hostels in Faro, I spent weeks looking for somewhere to rent. There was little for long-term rent since so much property was earmarked for short-term holiday lets. Eventually I found a flat in a renovated terraced house. It felt light and spacious and had a patio area at the back, open to the sky and equipped with a barbecue. From my balcony on the day I moved in I could see nine storks perched on various buildings, including two churches. Their presence, complete with the usual clattering of bills, felt warm and welcoming.

I took in my new surroundings. My narrow street had terraced houses on either side and I stepped out of my front door onto a raised pavement of cobbles with a stone step leading down to the road. The district had the air of old Portugal, but with the odd modern touch. A minute's walk away was a time capsule, with "messages and memories of the life and thinking of our age" stored away in 2019 to be reopened in 2220. Just beyond the time capsule was an 18th century Baroque church with the skulls and bones of Carmelite monks. In front of the church, in a square, traders gathered on Sunday to sell local produce, from Algarve orange honey to mangos. A man with a brown dog perched serenely on his left shoulder sometimes sat and played the accordion for the benefit of shoppers.

After moving in, armed with my rental contract, I went to the Town Hall and requested the right to reside in Portugal for five years. I did this on 3 February 2020, the first working day after Britain left the European Union. Because Britain was still in a transition period with the EU I was treated as an EU citizen and I marvelled at how easy it was for me to acquire temporary residency. I handed over 15 euros to a friendly woman bureaucrat and that was that.

The flat was unfurnished so another priority was acquiring some essential items. I just had time to take delivery of a Moroccan carpet, beds, a table and a sofa when shops shut and normal life came to a halt. The first sign in my world that COVID-19 was a game-changing disease was the new way of shopping for food. At my local store, I arrived one day to find a queue stretching outside.

A woman allowed shoppers to enter in small groups. The Sunday market closed and I took the hint. This was serious.

On 19 March 2020 Portugal introduced a state of emergency, the first since the Carnation Revolution. There is a clarity and crispness about a state of emergency. It was approved by parliament, felt democratic and after its introduction the Portuguese moved like starlings in flight into a new dance with the world. Of course there wasn't actually much movement. This was a lockdown and people stayed indoors unless there was a legal reason to go out, such as buying food. But the analogy sprang to mind because the shift in behaviour felt like a collective endeavour. I saw no panic buying and the sense of social cohesion was palpable.

Suddenly Faro was dead. The Chelsea café, my favourite haunt for cheesecake, closed its doors, as did all the bars and eateries. I'd had no time to make friends but I bonded with Faro, hugged it as best I could, and regularly walked to the sea. The marina and a tidal lagoon were just minutes away. Smelling the sea, tuning in to the shoreline sights of the day, all of this was a sweet change from my flat. I walked out on a jetty, binoculars in hand, and scanned the mudflats when the tide was out. Little things gave such pleasure, like watching three spoonbills fly in to land while I was focused on a heron feeding. Scuttling crabs added to the sense of the non-human world doing business as usual. Some creatures did apparently change their habits. The skipper of an excursion boat told me that, during lockdown, dolphins in the seas off Faro realised that human beings had gone quiet and unusually for them swam closer to shore, into the lagoons.

In a lockdown we all follow our own path. I listened to lots of BBC Welsh-language radio, improving my Welsh. Like others I used technology to keep in touch with family and friends. One contact turned into a bit of comedy. A friend in Brazil asked if I could do a radio interview for a local station there on life under quarantine in Europe. Radio, he had said, so I chatted away sporting a month-old lockdown beard and a scruffy shirt. We spoke on Skype and I should have realised what was happening. I was on live television, looking like a tramp.

One theme that emerged at least in the early phase of the pandemic was that Portugal, buoyed by political and social cohesion, coped better than its neighbour with the challenge presented by the virus. In March, harrowing reports emerged from Spain of army units finding corpses abandoned in their beds at retirement homes. Spain's complex politics seemed to hamper efforts to ride the storm.

According to worldometers.info, by 31 December 2020 Spain had suffered 50,689 COVID-related deaths and Portugal 6,906, so 1,084 deaths per million in Spain and 678 in Portugal. Having earlier flirted with the cause of political union between the two countries, in 2020 I drew the conclusion that Portuguese control over its own affairs served it well. The Portugal-Spain border closed for three-and-a-half months.

COVID did nothing to unify Spain politically. The spats between left and right and between Madrid and Catalan separatists seemed to intensify. In one incident, the central government and some Catalans rowed over facemasks. Madrid sent 1,714,000 masks to Catalonia and some angry separatists there accused the central government of making a coded reference to the fall of Barcelona at the end of a war in 1714. In Spain, the pandemic highlighted the historic lack of a strong political centre and the gaping divide between left and right.

Portugal's Socialist government operated in a very different environment and political peace reigned. What struck me was the efficiency and stoicism of the Portuguese. In the supermarket where I shopped, public announcements told shoppers to keep their distance and tapes on the floor at checkout indicated where people should stand. The workers at the tills went behind plastic shields. COVID-19 was embraced in Faro's street art and a depiction of the virus stretched over two terraced buildings.

In dozens of countries, the pandemic served as an excuse for governments to ride roughshod over human rights. Portugal won international plaudits from human rights campaigners for a move in the opposite opposition. In April 2020, so during lockdown, Portugal decided to temporarily grant full citizenship rights to all migrants and asylum seekers currently in the country. The aim was to ensure that everyone had access to healthcare.

We emerged from a six-week state of emergency on May 3 and moved into what was officially dubbed a "calamity". Wearing masks became compulsory in enclosed spaces. In May restaurants and cafés reopened and I headed to the Chelsea café for a happy reunion with cheesecake. Jacaranda trees, associated with rebirth, had burst into their blue-purple bloom in the city. One day I saw a stork flying over jacarandas close to the Faro marina and my heart sang.

Of course the pandemic hammered Portugal's tourism-dependent economy which shrank by 7.6 percent in 2020, the sharpest annual fall since 1936. Measured in terms of bed-nights, Portuguese tourism was knocked back to levels last seen in 1993. When the government introduced a new state of emergency in November, because of the rising incidence of COVID, the mood in the Algarve was fractured. On Saturday November 21, when Faro had a curfew from 1 p.m., several hundred people, many from the tourism sector and the arts, staged an anti-lockdown protest. A sculpture of a red heart expressing love for Faro was draped with a photomontage showing a mask-wearing waiter carrying drinks. The waiter was depicted hanging from a noose and the caption read "We want to breathe."

Tourism was not helped by Britain's decision to keep Portugal on a quarantine blacklist for much of the year – Britons returning from Portugal had to self-isolate for two weeks. This decision infuriated Lisbon. Prime Minister Boris Johnson, sick with COVID in April and hovering between life and death, had been cared for by a team that included a Portuguese male nurse. The dynamics of all this seemed to fit into the centuries-long history of unequal Anglo-Portuguese partnership.

The mood at the start of 2021 felt brittle and suddenly Portugal suffered a dramatic reverse. The country headed into a second lockdown and briefly endured the highest rates of new infections in the world. It was now harder hit than Spain. The Portuguese government blamed the soaring death toll on the coronavirus variant first found in Britain and acknowledged that relaxed restrictions over Christmas had contributed.

By the second lockdown, the Algarve really felt the economic pain. Now beggars occasionally knocked at my door pleading for funds, something that never happened when I first moved to Faro. Algarve's food bank provided vital supplies for 29,000 people, nearly double the number before COVID restrictions.

Portugal will surely bounce back. It remains a magnet for a great diversity of people. So, to end, here are three vignettes from the plague year of 2020 that give some flavour of Portugal's cosmopolitan vibe and switch the spotlight to happier themes.

In mid-January, on a train from Faro to the west Algarve town of Lagos, I conversed with a French-speaking man called Fahmi. His parents were Tunisian but he had lived mostly in France. In 2019 he walked from France along the pilgrim route to Santiago de Compostela in north-west Spain. From there he continued south to Sagres, covering about 2,500 kilometres in two months. So we had both walked to Sagres!

We enjoyed one of those easy, free-flowing conversations that can happen with strangers and discussed everything from the challenges in the Arab world to the future of Portugal. I learned that he too, after his long walk, had decided to settle in Portugal. He was on his way to the area of Aljezur, where I had met the Swiss sea captain, to try to buy land. He talked about acquiring teepees and yurts and his whole vision was to create a community. Fahmi, a stocky man probably in his late thirties, projected confidence and purpose, physical and spiritual strength. I found it easy to imagine those yurts going up and the community becoming real. Fahmi predicted that many more foreigners would move to Portugal, which he saw as the centre of a healing energy. To my surprise, he introduced into our conversation the ancient super-continent of Pangaea that began to break apart about 175 million years ago.

"If you look at a map of Pangaea, Portugal is right in the middle of it," said Fahmi. I perused a map later and he is correct. Portugal snuggled cosily against what is now Greenland. The geology of the Algarve reflects the break-up of Pangaea and cliffs in the west, where Fahmi wanted to settle, contain fossilised coral, reminders of a distant age.

The second vignette is a sailing expedition, in October, from the Algarve port of Olhão to the Spanish resort of Chipiona. Four of us sailed in a 12.5m long boat, the *Blue Swan*, a lovingly restored vessel built in 1976. Our Portuguese skipper, Ricardo, was a bearded handsome hunk who combined nautical skill with affability and charm. The crew consisted of a warm Italian journalist, Carla, a Russian woman called Masha, and myself. Masha, who worked in Lisbon as a human rights activist, was well-travelled and regaled us with accounts of walking in remote Kamchatka. After months with little social contact, the conversations felt like the soft patter of rain after prolonged drought.

The language on board was English and I had it easy because I was the only one with English as mother tongue. But when Ricardo gave the crisp instruction "Masha, hoist the main sail", Masha did precisely that. I was the oldest on board and hardly pulled my weight. But I did turns in the galley, preparing a leek and chestnut risotto and frying tuna caught by Ricardo, the freshest and tastiest I have eaten.

We were away for four days and the highlight was a 13-hour night sail that brought us all the way home from Chipiona in one uninterrupted voyage. The moon was perhaps three-quarters full. On watch with Masha, I sat and watched the moonlight shimmering on the waves and the sky bursting with stars. The heavenly bodies imparted a bizarre feeling of being held, even though they were above me, not below me. When not on watch I tried to sleep on my bunk in the bow. The boat crashed through the waves and my bunk felt like a surfboard. The voyage was an extraordinary assault on the senses. But in a testing year, it was also an experience of companionship and adventure that fed my soul.

A final vignette. One headline story for me in the plague year was a decision by an old friend to come and winter not far away. Guy Dinmore, also a journalist and a Welshman, has a great fondness for both Portugal and the sea, so he came to live for a while by the Algarve shore. In the siege-like atmosphere that prevailed during the pandemic, we provided support for one another. Guy coined the lovely phrase "to close ranks and open bottles" which neatly describes the convivial spirit of our meetings.

The bottles we opened tended to contain wine, but on one of our get-togethers Bacchus played no role whatsoever and the day had a special character all its own. On December 21, to mark the Great Conjunction of Jupiter and Saturn, Guy and I went to a meditation on a beach. Nine of us in all, from Britain, Belgium and the Netherlands, gathered by the seashore in the friendly fishing town of Fuseta. For astrologers, the conjunction was a very big event, heralding the lighter energy of a new Aquarian age and evolutionary leaps for humanity. Gregg, a gentle young man from Birmingham, came around our little circle offering everyone a waft of burning sage, held in a seashell. He then walked round our group, soon after sunset, beating on a goatskin drum before we fell into a silent meditation. Jupiter and Saturn, looking to the naked eye like one bright star, hung high in the sky above the wispiest of clouds. At the edge of the water, the silhouette of Fuseta's disused lifeboat station, standing on stilts, interrupted the line of a gentle orange glow at the close of day.

Bibliography

Boxer, C.R. *The Portuguese Seaborne Empire 1415-1825.* London: Pelican Books, 1973

Cavalcanti (Filho), José Paulo. *Fernando Pessoa: uma quase-autobiographia.* Porto: Porto Editora, 2011.

Cliff, Nigel. *The Last Crusade, The Epic Voyages of Vasco da Gama.* HarperCollins, 2012

Crowley, Roger. *Conquerors: How Portugal Forged the First Global Empire.* London: Faber and Faber, 2016

Disney, Anthony. *A History of Portugal and the Portuguese Empire (two volumes).* Cambridge, UK: Cambridge University Press, 2009.

Hatton, Barry. *The Portuguese.* Lisbon: Clube do Autor, 2012

Hatton, Barry. *Queen of the Sea, A History of Lisbon.* London: C. Hurst & Co, 2018.

Nogueira, Manuela. *O Meu Tio Fernando Pessoa.* V.N. Famaliçao, Portugal: Centro Atlântico, 2015.

Page, Martin. *The First Global Village, How Portugal Changed the World.* Alfragide, Portugal: Casa das Letras, 2002

Pessoa, Fernando. *The Book of Disquiet,* London: Serpent's Tail, 1991.

Saramago, José. *Journey to Portugal: A Pursuit of Portugal's History and Culture.* London: The Harvill Press, 2002.

Acknowledgements

My thanks go first to the spirit and people of Portugal for motivating me to write this book. I am grateful to all those who took the time to converse with me during my walk. They included Viriato Morais, Paulo Duarte, Father Agostinho Ramalho Pereira, Isabel Miliciano, Professor Aurora Carapinha, Jorge Rosa, Ricardo and Carolina Romero, Sandra Santos and Friedrich Germann.

Guy Dinmore provided great support at every stage, from advice on places to visit, including the old Sufi fortress on the coast, to proofreading the final manuscript. Val Poore was a wonderful encourager and she beta read the text, offering important editorial counsel.

Enya Holland at SilverWood Books gave feedback on an early partial draft and professional guidance throughout the whole process of getting a book out into the world.

I'd also like to thank Carla Chelo, Nick Daubeny, Suzie Greenwood, Eduarda Johnson, Alecia McKenzie, Fabiana Mendes, Chris Phillips, Laurence Purcell, Aidan Reynolds, John Tranmer and Isabel Winstanley for advice, encouragement or sometimes challenge.

I'm very grateful to my daughters Rachel and Megan for once again providing illustrations for a travel book of mine. Megan also kindly furnished a map showing my route.

The Wider World of Memoirs

If you would like to chat with the author and other memoir authors and readers, do join the friendly, fun Facebook group, We Love Memoirs. https://www.facebook.com/groups/welovememoirs/

Index